Building Southwark

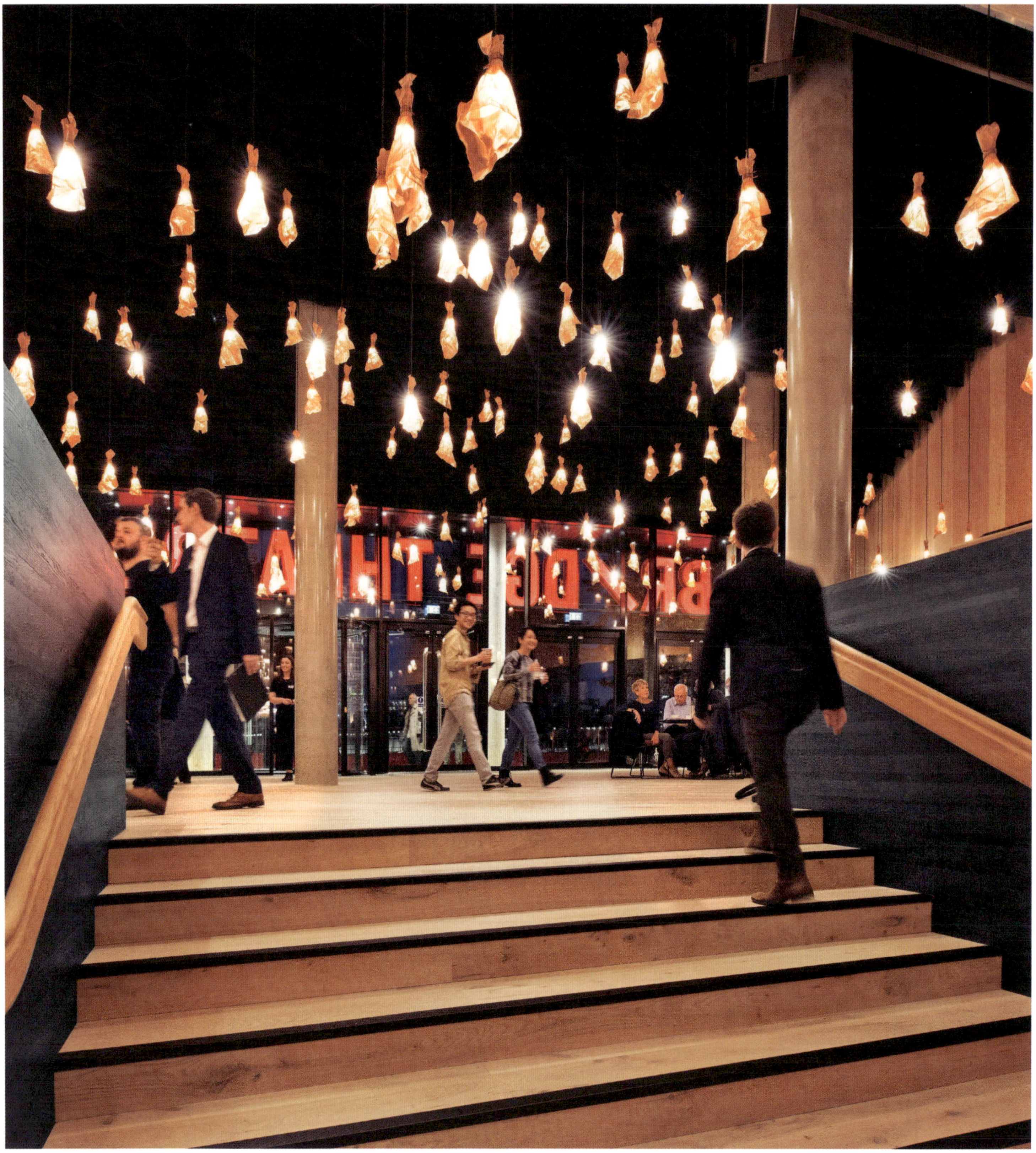

Merrell Publishers is grateful to the following sponsors for their generous support, which has made this book possible:

Building Southwark

Architecture & Regeneration in a London Borough

Kenneth Powell

Contents

6 Foreword by Lord Foster

7 Foreword by Cllr Kieron Williams

8 Introduction

Culture and Leisure

18 Camberwell Library

20 Canada Water Library

22 Castle Centre

24 Mountview

26 Southwark Town Hall and Theatre Peckham

28 Siobhan Davies Dance Studios

30 Southwark Park Pavilion

32 Blavatnik Building, Tate Modern

34 Una Marson Library

Housing

38 95 Peckham Road

40 Albion Street Housing

42 Appleby Blue

44 Chapter London Bridge

46 Aylesbury Estate Block SO1 and Harriet Hardy Extra Care

50 London Square

54 Manor Place Housing

56 Neo Bankside

58 One Blackfriars

60 One the Elephant

62 Royal Road Housing

63 Stead Street Housing

64 Two Fifty One

66 81–87 Weston Street

Infrastructure & Jobs

70 53 and 55 Great Suffolk Street

72 Employment Academy

74 Guy's Cancer Centre

76 Harold Moody Health Centre

78 The Hithe

80 London Bridge Station

82 King's College Hospital Campus

84 160 Tooley Street

86 Walworth Town Hall and Central Library

Mixed Use

- 90   Bankside Yards
- 92   Blackfriars Circus
- 94   Elephant and Castle Town Centre
- 96   Nunhead Green
- 98   Southbank Tower
- 100 Maple Quays and Ontario Point
- 104 The Shard Quarter
    - The Shard
    - News Building
    - Shard Place

Education

- 110 ARK All Saints Academy, Highshore School and St Michael's Church
- 111 Rotherhithe Primary School
- 112 Bellenden Primary School
- 113 SILS3 Pupil Referral Unit
- 114 Cherry Garden School
- 115 Newlands Academy
- 116 Phoenix Primary School
- 117 Spa School
- 118 Dulwich College Laboratory
- 120 Haberdashers' Borough Academy
- 122 Clarence Centre for Enterprise and Innovation, LSBU
- 124 LSBU Hub
- 128 Southwark College
- 130 Camberwell College of Arts

Landscape

- 134 Elephant Park
    - The Tree House
    - Trafalgar Place
    - South Gardens
- 140 Canada Water Masterplan
- 142 Burgess Park
- 144 One Tower Bridge and Potters Fields Park
- 146 Dickens' Fields

- 148 Sponsors
- 148 Index
- 151 Acknowledgements
- 151 Picture Credits

Foreword

Norman Foster, Founder and Executive Chairman,
Foster + Partners

In recent years we have witnessed a rapid pace of change across London. At the beginning of this decade, the city's population had risen by 1.8 million since 2005 – more than the combined population increases for both Paris and New York in the same period. I have often called London an analogue city, rather than a digital one such as New York. The structure of the city, with its absence of grids and numerical references, is more organic, having evolved out of individual villages that have developed and coalesced over time. The streets, squares and plazas – the infrastructure of the city or its 'urban glue', as I like to refer to it – are what holds the city together.

It was this inimitable spirit that underpinned the design of the Millennium Bridge, which has been a great social equalizer for the city and played an integral role in the extraordinary transformation of the London borough of Southwark. Linking the City and St Paul's Cathedral with the Globe Theatre and Tate Modern on Bankside, the crossing immediately dissolved the boundary between north and south and kick-started the revival of this long-neglected district. The project far exceeded expectations, increasing the value of property and paving the way for 60 new hotels, while quickly doubling both the estimated 4 million crossings per year and the 1,500 new jobs that were initially forecast for Southwark.

This pioneering venture would never have been possible without the protagonists, who had the remarkable vision to conceive it in the first place. Principal among them, Sir David Bell, chairman of the Millennium Bridge Trust; Sir Stuart Lipton, who played a key role in the negotiations between the City and Southwark; Dr Savas Sivetidis, who was the head of planning and regeneration at Southwark Council and subsequently director of the Cross River Partnership; and Dame Judith Mayhew Jonas, who chaired both the Policy and Resources Committee at the Corporation of the City of London and the Cross River Partnership. The commissioning body worked tirelessly to achieve funding, realize our design to the highest possible standard, and set up a charity to maintain the crossing for future generations. Obstacles that once loomed large were overcome by their unwavering commitment and philanthropic support.

Similarly, our ongoing project at 18 Blackfriars Road reflects an ambition to build and strengthen communities in Southwark – and demonstrates how close collaboration with the planning authority and key stakeholders can bring profound and far-reaching public benefits. Spearheaded by Hines and Lipton Rogers, this landmark project will transform a 0.8-hectare brownfield site – that has remained undeveloped for twenty years – into a thriving new neighbourhood. The project will bring a wealth of social benefits to the city by providing new homes, offices, retail, and a range of cultural and community facilities. New public spaces will join up with a cycle highway and public transport interchanges to encourage car-free travel across London.

With sustainability at its heart, the development is designed to be fossil fuel-free, 100 per cent electric and Net Zero Carbon in operation, with 95 per cent of the site's heat demand served by ground-source heat pumps that share, store and offset energy. A 150 per cent increase in biodiversity is also planned for the site, including the planting of one hundred new trees. A new sustainable exemplar for Southwark and a distinctive new destination for London, 18 Blackfriars will offer spaces to live, work and play for everyone.

Both these projects are united by a desire to reconnect the urban fabric, bring people together, and breathe further life into Southwark. Furthermore, they have both been driven by bold and visionary client and planning teams, who embrace the spirit of regeneration. They highlight the role design and teamwork can play in enhancing the quality of life for all, and are symbolic of the ongoing revival of London's South Bank. We have good reasons to be highly optimistic about London's future, as it continues to be a city that is unafraid to embrace the power of change for good.

Foreword

Councillor Kieron Williams, Leader of Southwark Council

The spaces around us have a profound impact on our lives. Our homes, schools, workplaces and public spaces all shape us. Good design can make them healthier, more inclusive, more inspiring and more joyful, and in so doing it can transform lives.

In Southwark we have for many years placed high-quality design at the heart of our approach. On the following pages you can see some of the results: the parks, homes, workplaces and public buildings that we have shaped, and the benefits they have brought for our whole community.

We've seen how the landmark projects that were delivered on Bankside some twenty-five years ago – including Tate Modern and the Millennium Bridge – have opened up and redefined our stretch of the Thames. They brought new life, culture, jobs and commerce, and made Southwark a global destination.

Since then, good planning and architecture have transformed other neighbourhoods in our borough. Take a walk through Burgess Park and you will see how good design can transform lives. Fourteen years ago it was a space the community had turned its back on. Today it is a true people's park, full of people from every walk of life strolling, BMXing, fishing, barbecuing, exercising, playing or just relaxing, and with a wealth of new biodiversity and overlooked by hundreds of new council homes.

That is not the only part of our borough that has been renewed. Elephant and Castle has a new public park and leisure centre, with a new Northern line station and a new home for London College of Communication under construction. Canada Water is also being rejuvenated, with its iconic library and dock complete with wetlands; the TEDI engineering school; another leisure centre under construction; and new housing, retail, leisure and public spaces all coming forward.

The schemes featured in this book are just a few highlights of the last twenty years of development. It could easily have featured another fifty or more. While several high-profile and prize-winning projects are included, they sit alongside others that might be less eye-catching but are every bit as important to our borough.

I'm particularly proud of the schools we have built over the last two decades, from the fabulous SILS3 for inclusive learning, to the stunning Rotherhithe Primary School. The quality of our school buildings is a vital component of a good education, lifting aspirations and improving attainment. It is those children who, given a good start in life and educated in our wonderful collection of new schools, will go on to drive the next twenty years of improvements in Southwark, London, the UK and beyond.

Southwark: a collection of urban villages, looking across to the Thames.

Introduction

The year 2025 marks Southwark's sixtieth birthday, the modern borough having come into existence in 1965 with the merger of the boroughs of Bermondsey, Camberwell and Southwark under a new local authority. The old boroughs were formally designated only in 1900. At that time the ancient Southwark – 'the borough', a medieval suburb of the City of London – merged with an urban area that, swallowing up such villages as Rotherhithe and Dulwich, was largely a product of the previous century. The new borough had a population of nearly half a million, many living in an environment described as 'a brick jungle'.

The last half-century has brought radical change, with the industries that were dominant within living memory largely vanished, along with the docks that serviced them. Whole quarters of the borough were flattened by bombs in the Second World War, opening the way for a heroic programme of renewal that focused on the provision of new housing. Not all of it was as successful as the Brandon estate in Kennington, with its mix of towers and lower-rise buildings, including renovated Victorian terraces. Of the massive Aylesbury estate, *The Buildings of England* commented: 'an exploration can only be recommended for those who enjoy being stunned by the impersonal megalomaniac creations of the mid C20'. The Heygate estate, completed in 1974, was equally stolid – and best seen from a distance.

By the 1980s commercial development had begun to transform Bankside. The Kuwaiti-funded London Bridge City of that decade was extended in the early twenty-first century by Foster + Partners' More London, with nearly 280,000 square metres of office space as well as City Hall, the headquarters of the Greater London Authority until 2021. The transformation of Bankside was completed in spectacular fashion in 2012 by the Shard (page 104), Britain's tallest building, containing offices, a hotel and flats, designed by RPBW and part of a comprehensive development of land around London Bridge station. SimpsonHaugh's One Blackfriars (page 58) is another landmark on the river, a fifty-storey residential tower 170 metres tall and memorable in form, the principal element in a mixed-use development containing a hotel, shops and restaurants. Tall buildings remain a contentious subject in London. Richard Seifert's King's Reach Tower was controversial back in the 1970s; curtailed in height by the planners, it never functioned well as an office building and was seen as a clumsy addition to the skyline. KPF's radical reconstruction as the Southbank Tower (page 98), increasing the height of the structure as part of a conversion to residential use, has given the building a new elegance of form as well as integrating it into its context.

Proposals for tall (that is, over 30 metres) buildings in Southwark are nothing new; local-authority housing developments of the 1960s around Old Kent Road include towers up to twenty-one storeys high. But the Council's policy, developed in the context of the 2021 London Plan, is to concentrate the development of new tall buildings in three zones: a large area extending from Elephant and Castle to the riverside, where the Shard forms a marker and the towers of the City are close at hand; the area along the Old Kent Road, with its existing high-rise housing estates; and Canada Water, an area of intensive renewal. The large area extending southwards – Peckham, Nunhead, Camberwell, Dulwich, with low-rise nineteenth-century housing a dominant feature – is clearly a zone where proposals for tall buildings would not generally be welcomed.

Elephant and Castle is undergoing a transformation in which tall buildings feature prominently. The insightful critic Ian Nairn, writing in 1964, when the redevelopment of the area (which had been devastated by wartime bombing) was underway, wrote: 'what has been completed so far has varying architectural quality but all of it looks as though architecture was a Deadly Serious Business; it has no give or bounce. This is not a hopeful sign, especially in a place as Cockney as this.' Twenty years later *The Buildings of England* used such adjectives as 'tortuous', 'ruthless' and 'depressing' to describe the 1960s architecture of 'the Elephant', commenting that 'the comfort of

Foster + Partners' scheme at 18 Blackfriars Road will create a new mixed-use quarter on the banks of the River Thames.

pedestrians had very low priority'. Southwark's regeneration programme for the area, launched in 2010 and extending into the next decade, provided for comprehensive renewal of the area, with 5,000 new homes, a pedestrianized town centre, new retail and leisure space, and generous parks and open spaces. New housing includes towers of forty or more storeys, in line with the London Plan. Squire & Partners' One the Elephant (37 storeys, 284 flats; page 60) and Allies and Morrison's Two Fifty One (41 storeys, 335 flats; page 64) are examples. Major improvements to public transport address the increased density of population.

The riverside, with the context of the Shard to address, provides scope for exceptionally tall buildings. The ongoing Bankside Yards development at Blackfriars (page 90) includes a fifty-storey residential tower in the context of an innovative mixed-use project. Foster + Partners' 18 Blackfriars Road project, which received planning consent in 2024, provides for three towers, the tallest at forty-five storeys, containing offices as part of a mammoth mixed-use scheme that includes two residential high rises. The housing tower at Blackfriars Circus by Maccreanor Lavington (page 92) is one element in a scheme that includes lower-rise housing and seeks to repair the damaged urban fabric around St George's Circus. KPF's Chapter tower (page 44) near London Bridge station is designed as a self-contained student village thirty-nine storeys high. The regeneration of Canada Water, powered by a partnership between Southwark Council and British Land, has generated new high-rise residential buildings designed by Howells and by Allies and Morrison (pages 100 and 140), both notable for their careful integration into a new townscape.

Southwark Council is the biggest local-authority social landlord in London and the fourth biggest nationally. (A report in 2020 found that half the households in the borough had an annual income of less than £30,000.) In response to the demand for affordable housing, in 2013 the Council set an ambitious target of providing 11,000 new council homes by 2043.

This programme must be seen in the context of the massive programme of replacement for the failed housing developments of the 1960s and 70s. The Aylesbury estate in Walworth contained more than 2,700 homes. The process of demolition and replacement has more than a decade still to run, but when completed it will provide 4,200 new homes, 580 of them rented on an affordable basis. A masterplan by HTA Design provides for the complete demolition of the estate, with its failed concept of 'streets in the sky', and the creation of a new urban landscape reflecting the existing context of the surrounding streets and squares. Parks and gardens are slotted into the renewed urban quarter.

The Heygate estate, close to Elephant and Castle, was another heroic development (of more than 1,200 homes) that eventually failed and was demolished in 2010–14 as part of the far-reaching programme of development at the Elephant. Its site has now largely been developed through a partnership between Southwark Council and Lendlease. The new quarter, Elephant Park (page 134), will provide more than 2,500 homes, around 25 per cent of which will be classed as affordable, alongside offices and retail space and a new park. Trafalgar Place, the first element in the masterplan to be completed (in 2015 – architect dRMM; pages 136–8), provides a radical contrast to the demolished estate, with a mix of buildings ranging in scale from four to ten storeys and containing 235 homes, 25 per cent of them affordable.

Alongside large-scale new housing developments, Southwark's drive to deliver new homes has generated a number of projects that are modest in scale but contribute to the architectural diversity of the borough. The development at Royal Road (architect: Panter Hudspith; page 62) was completed in 2013 by Affinity Sutton Homes (now merged with Clarion Housing Group) as part of Southwark's Early Housing Sites (EHS) initiative to provide rehousing options for displaced Heygate tenants. It provides ninety-six affordable homes, 80 per cent of them rented, in a project that fits comfortably into the townscape, its well-detailed brick exterior providing a contrast to other EHS schemes where lightweight cladding systems were the norm. Even more modest in scale is Bell Phillips' development at Albion Street (page 40) – just twenty-six homes for social and intermediate rent slotted in between two listed churches in Rotherhithe and including a new public square. AOC Architecture's housing at Nunhead Green (just fourteen units; page 96) is playful in form but part of a remarkable process of urban repair that includes a community centre and the Green itself, rescued from neglect to become a heavily used local amenity.

On a much larger scale, the London Square development (architects: Allford Hall Monaghan Morris and Coffey Architects; page 50) in Bermondsey took as its starting point a run-down industrial site that retained some buildings of local historic interest. The project provides more than 400 new homes – a third of them affordable/social units – along with new quarters for the arts organizations based there. The judges for the 2021 RIBA Awards described Peter Barber's housing at 95 Peckham Road (page 38), essentially a reinvention of the traditional London mansion block, as 'the work of an architect who knows how to make housing design a success, but with a sense of humour thrown into the mix … the new block is vibrant and alive, making a very positive contribution to the urban realm.'

Barber's second completed project in Southwark, commissioned by the charity

Thames Reach, refurbished and converted a listed Edwardian building, formerly council offices – also on Peckham Road – as a training and support centre for the long-term unemployed, with historic interiors carefully restored (page 72). A new wing was added, replacing a dull office wing, another virtuoso exercise in the use of brick, with an open courtyard at its heart.

After new housing, education and training form perhaps the most significant element in Southwark's extraordinarily rich development programme. A remarkable programme of school-building took place in the borough during the two decades after the Second World War, with commissions to such practices as Lyons Israel Ellis, Stirling and Gowan, and Chamberlin, Powell & Bon alongside the work of the LCC's and GLC's school architects. Southwark was a significant beneficiary of the Building Schools for the Future programme launched by the Labour government in 2005, and the last twenty years have brought a renewed effort at school-building. Phoenix Primary School (page 116) in Bermondsey opened in 1967 and was listed Grade II forty years later. The brief to John Pardey Architects was to provide accommodation for an enlarged roll while respecting its unique character (the school was designed by the practice of David and Mary Medd, who had worked on the acclaimed Hertfordshire schools programme). Pardey's project of 2010 protected the unique plan, with single-storey pavilions arranged around a central garden/play area, while using a former parking area as the site for new

Much new housing in Southwark (shown here: Panter Hudspith Architects' project at Royal Road) is low- to medium-rise, contrasting with high-rise apartment blocks.

buildings. Sadly, the former classrooms were judged inadequate and have been repurposed as 'resource spaces' but left intact. The nearby Spa School (page 117) is another school that has undergone a sensitive expansion, with a memorable new addition, designed by AOC, subtly referring to the neighbouring Victorian board school but drawing on Post-modernist inspiration for its form and generous use of colour inside and out.

Southwark's SEND programme – catering for children with special educational needs and disabilities – has been designed to end the need to educate many of those pupils in special schools outside the borough. Newlands Academy (page 115), also in Peckham, designed for the needs of SEND and specifically for pupils with serious behavioural problems, is a skilful project that combines security, subtly handled, with a sense of openness and welcome. A holistic approach to the education of those with special needs equally underpins Hawkins\Brown's Cherry Garden School (page 114) in Peckham; catering for just eighty-five pupils, it reflects Southwark's ongoing commitment to young people who would find it a challenge to adapt to the life of a conventional school.

The academy programme has had a significant impact on secondary education in London, and there are a number of academies in Southwark. ARK All Saints Academy (page 110) in Camberwell, designed by Allford Hall Monaghan Morris, opened in 2014. An initiative from Southwark Council brought Mountview, one of Britain's leading drama schools, founded in 1945, to the borough from north London. Its new home (page 24), on what was a brownfield site close to Will Alsop's Peckham Library, is a tough 'warehouse for the arts' designed by architect Turner Works and opened in 2018. With 400 students, it is in the Creative Enterprise Zone designated by Southwark in 2018, encouraging the creation of employment possibilities for local people and the growth of performing arts in Southwark. Turner Works was also responsible for Peckham Levels, a groundbreaking conversion of a multistorey car park on Rye Lane into a hugely

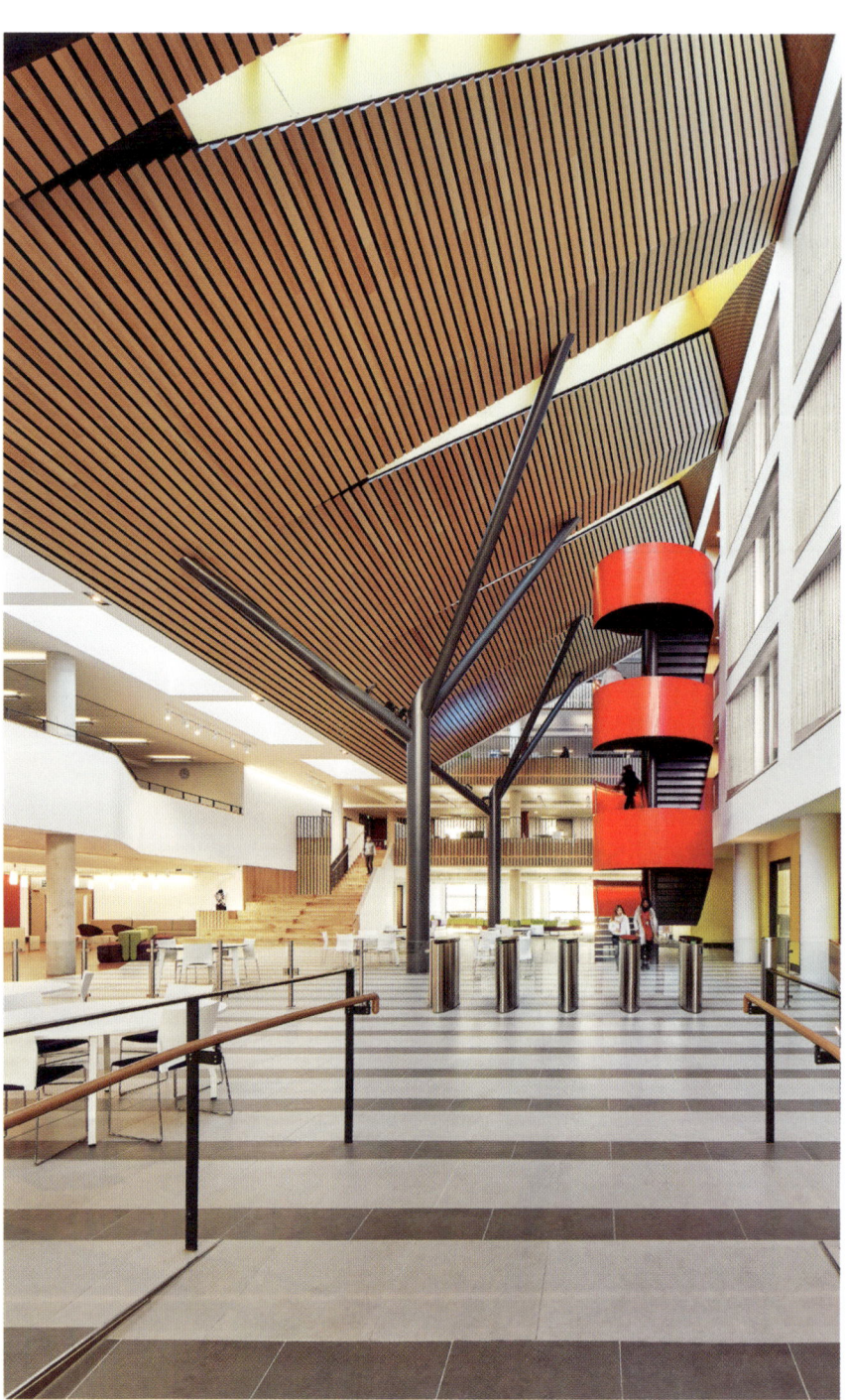

Southwark College's campus on The Cut has been transformed with a radical mix of refurbishment and new construction.

popular music and performing arts venue providing studio space for the creative arts; it opened in 2017 following an ideas competition launched by the Council in 2015.

Southwark gained its first university in 1992, when the former Polytechnic of the South Bank (founded in 1892) became South Bank University (now formally London South Bank University). The university's Hub (page 124) is close to Elephant and Castle, where it inherited a complex designed by the GLC Architects' Department and completed in 1976. The university's principal building on the London Road site, externally anonymous in appearance, was in urgent need of updating, with failing services and poor thermal performance. WilkinsonEyre's radical 'deep renovation' of the building, completed in 2022, faced some constraints; natural ventilation, for example, was ruled out because of the building's proximity to heavily trafficked roads. An updated mechanical system, with façades replaced to limit solar gain, has greatly improved the building's environmental performance. The new library is the most impressive space in a building that has been radically transformed into a symbol of the university's aspirations. Not far away, at St George's Circus, LSBU slotted in its Clarence Centre for Enterprise and Innovation (page 122) behind a terrace of long-derelict Georgian houses that had faced demolition before being listed Grade II in 2000. Surviving shopfronts and a former pub were retained and restored. The project (architect: Rivington Street Studio) sets a high standard for the integration of historic buildings into a new development that is part of the reinstatement of the damaged townscape around St George's Circus.

Southwark College, established in the 1990s with the merger of seven existing institutions, is one of Britain's leading further-education colleges. It, too, inherited a 1970s complex of buildings, deteriorating in condition with dated services and poor environmental performance – although on a prime site on The Cut. The radical refurbishment of the principal building (page 128) gave it a new heart in the form of an atrium that acts as the focus of the site. Other buildings were demolished and replaced by new blocks of between five and seven storeys wrapping around the atrium and housing the college's media and creative arts departments.

Public libraries have been the victim in many parts of Britain, including London, of spending cuts forced on local authorities. Southwark, however, has bucked the trend, opening a series of new libraries across the borough, with Will Alsop's Stirling Prize-winning Peckham Library leading the way and six new libraries opened since 2010. CZWG's Canada Water Library (page 20) is part of the large-scale renewal of the area, a reinvention of an institution with Victorian roots, with a café and performance space as well as books on offer. The Una Marson Library (page 34), part of the renewal of the Aylesbury estate site in Walworth, equally is not simply a place for reading; it contains a multipurpose community space and meeting rooms, as well as the library proper, in a visually striking space. Camberwell Library (page 18), opened in 2016 on Camberwell Green and designed by John McAslan + Partners, provides meeting and study spaces as well as books – and user numbers have more than doubled since its completion.

The repurposing of the former town hall on Peckham Road, a relatively undistinguished building no longer required by Southwark Council, converted and extended by Jestico + Whiles, provided much-needed accommodation for students at Goldsmiths (page 26). Intrinsic to the project was the opening on the site of Theatre Peckham, with a 200-seat auditorium, rehearsal space and a dance studio, and an agenda strongly slanted towards young people, with classes in dance, acting and music and a programme aimed at supporting new leaders in the performing arts.

The renaissance of Southwark has been underpinned by major developments in public transport. The extension of the Underground's Jubilee line and the London Overground drove the development of Canada Water and Bermondsey. London Bridge station, which even Sir John Betjeman – a lover of Victorian architecture – found hard to defend, was transformed by a £1 billion redevelopment that gave it a light-filled ground-level concourse with escalators accessing the platforms, a radical change from the 'tortuous' experience of using the station described by Betjeman. The station was once an impervious mass; now it connects areas of Southwark that it once simply overshadowed.

Not far from London Bridge, on the side of the Thames, Tate Modern, once a redundant and unloved power station, has emerged as one of the world's leading art museums. The conversion of the building by the Swiss architectural practice Herzog & de Meuron was completed in 2000, with the spectacular turbine hall as its centrepiece.

Between 2007 and 2016 the former switch house at the rear of the building was replaced by the Blavatnik Building (page 32), a strikingly sculptural eleven-storey addition set on top of the power station's oil tanks – themselves converted into dramatic gallery spaces.

Another major cultural gain – this one from the One Tower Bridge development (page 144) – was the opening in 2017 of the 900-seat Bridge Theatre, slotted into the base of an apartment block close to the bridge itself. Designed by architect Haworth Tompkins for the London Theatre Company (founded by Nicholas Hytner and Nick Starr), it is the city's first entirely new theatre in decades, and a key feature of a development that has created a new,

Sweeping roofs cover the platforms of the renewed London Bridge station.

More London and the Shard are symbols of the dynamic renewal of Southwark, with commercial development playing an important role. The building under construction is KPF's Chapter London Bridge (page 44).

mixed-use quarter on a site with a long and contentious history. Seating an audience of up to 1,100 via an innovative decking system, the theatre is designed to be fully flexible, allowing performances in a number of formats but always providing the immediacy and intimacy that were key to the brief. Timber is used extensively to create a space that is warm and welcoming, but equally a place for conversation before the performance and during the interval.

With its striking form and prominent river frontage, Tate Modern has become a symbol of Southwark's emergence as a global cultural quarter, reinforced by the proximity of Shakespeare's Globe theatre and the Bridge Theatre, while Borough Market, close to Southwark Cathedral, is a vibrant visitor attraction. Fifty years ago the riverside was largely deserted, a place of decay following the demise of London's docks. Today the continuing renaissance of Southwark is summed up in the borough's motto, emblazoned on its coat of arms: 'United to serve'. Southwark is a destination for travellers from across the world, but equally a place where the lives of local people have been transformed and enriched by several decades of enlightened development.

Introduction

Culture and Leisure

The opening of Tate Modern in 2000 put Southwark on the global cultural map. It is Britain's most visited museum, attracting more than 4 million visitors in 2022, and the opening of the Blavatnik Building in 2016 was a spectacular addition. Southwark has become a focus of the art world, with numerous private galleries. The performing arts, too, have flourished in the borough, and drama and music feature strongly on the curriculum of Southwark's schools. The former town hall on Peckham Road has been repurposed as student housing, with a 200-seat theatre attached; the theatre has a particular focus on working with young people. Mountview in Peckham is one of Britain's leading drama schools, while the Siobhan Davies Dance Studios is a major centre for the training of dancers, with a strong programme of outreach to the local community.

'Airy, accessible, inspiring. I love the feel of the whole place – on my own or with friends and family.'

A REGULAR AT THE BLAVATNIK BUILDING, TATE MODERN

Camberwell Library

ARCHITECT John McAslan + Partners
DATE 2016
ADDRESS 48 Camberwell Green, SE5 7AL
CLIENT London Borough of Southwark

The site of the new Camberwell Library, commissioned by Southwark Council in 2012, is on the northeastern corner of Camberwell Green, at the heart of the community. The clear site – left vacant after wartime bombing that devastated the surrounding area – allowed the construction of a freestanding two-storey building standing in a new public space, with no 'back of house'. It has an open aesthetic, welcoming the public in to use its facilities, which include IT provision, a study room and meeting rooms used by local community groups.

The building is strongly contextual thanks to the light-coloured brick cladding, which responds to the aesthetic of neighbouring buildings, where London stock brick is predominant. The new public space surrounding the library, paved in silver-grey slabs, complements the architecture and forms a new pedestrian route to the Green and a link to nearby housing. Timber is used extensively inside to create a warm and welcoming space, generously daylit.

Sustainability was a key objective. The building lies close to a busy road, which is a heavily used bus route. Louvres for natural ventilation, controlled via the monitoring of internal air temperature and CO_2, incorporate a preheat element for use in cold weather, to eliminate cold draughts. A sedum roof was included in the environmental strategy, encouraging biodiversity through the carefully considered use of plants that are indigenous to the area. Low-energy lighting throughout is another element in the design strategy, further reducing running costs.

The library has become a heavily used local amenity. Its rational, undemonstrative architecture is clearly popular – at the time of writing, user numbers had doubled since it opened.

SITE PLAN

Culture and Leisure

The library is on Camberwell Green, at the heart of the local community, with a new public space linked to the Green itself. This highly sustainable building has become a valued amenity, with study and meeting rooms alongside the usual library facilities.

Culture and Leisure

Canada Water Library

ARCHITECT CZWG
DATE 2011
ADDRESS 21 Surrey Quays Road, SE16 7AR
CLIENT London Borough of Southwark

The late Will Alsop's Peckham Library, completed in 2000, was a sensational reinvention of a building type rooted in the late nineteenth century. It won the RIBA Stirling Prize that year. In the last two decades, when other local authorities have closed libraries, new libraries have opened in Southwark – the latest, the Una Marson Library (page 34), in early 2024.

The commission for the new library overlooking Canada Water, completed in 2011 and a component in a massive regeneration project, went to the practice of CZWG. (The firm has a notable history in Southwark; its China Wharf housing of 1988 on the Bermondsey riverside was listed Grade II in 2018.)

The site for the library at Canada Water is close to the Tube station, which was the key driver in the renewal of the area, and direct access is provided from the station. Remarkably, this was CZWG's first public building. The site was tight and the building, anything but arbitrary, responds dramatically in the form of an inverted pyramid with a steep 60-degree overhang to the water of the former dock, providing a generous, elevated, light-filled space at the top for books and readers. Shelves are arranged to create intimate spaces for the library's users, and

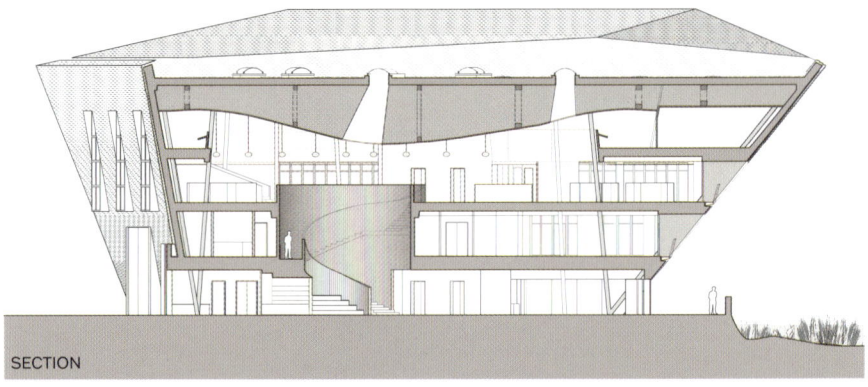
SECTION

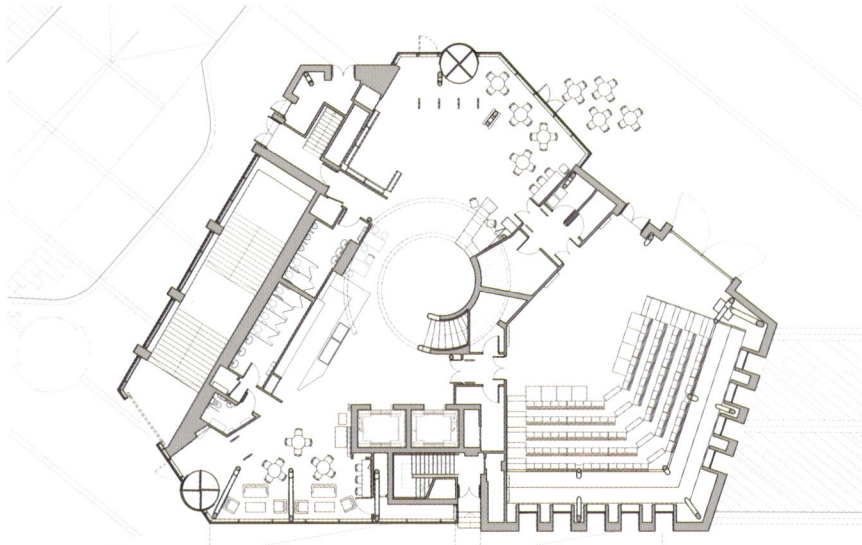
GROUND-FLOOR PLAN

a mezzanine provides a retreat for extended study. A wooden spiral staircase, supplemented by lifts, extends through the building. Below the top-floor reading room are staff offices and meeting rooms. The ground-floor reception area provides access to a café, which has become a very popular local venue, and to a well-used performance space. One doubts that the Victorians would have approved of this mix of activities – but attitudes to life and learning have changed.

The external treatment of the building, with its cladding of bronzed aluminium, is intended, in the words of CZWG partner Piers Gough, to look 'civic and grand without being pompous'. It succeeds. The building, which addresses a public square, holds its own as a strong statement of civic presence in a rapidly changing landscape.

Striking in form, the library is one element in the radical transformation of the quarter around Canada Water. Linked to the Underground station – itself a prime driver of regeneration – it is a new local landmark. The interior makes extensive use of timber and bold colour.

Culture and Leisure

Castle Centre

ARCHITECT John McAslan + Partners
DATE 2016
ADDRESS 2 St Gabriel Walk, SE1 6FG
CLIENT London Borough of Southwark

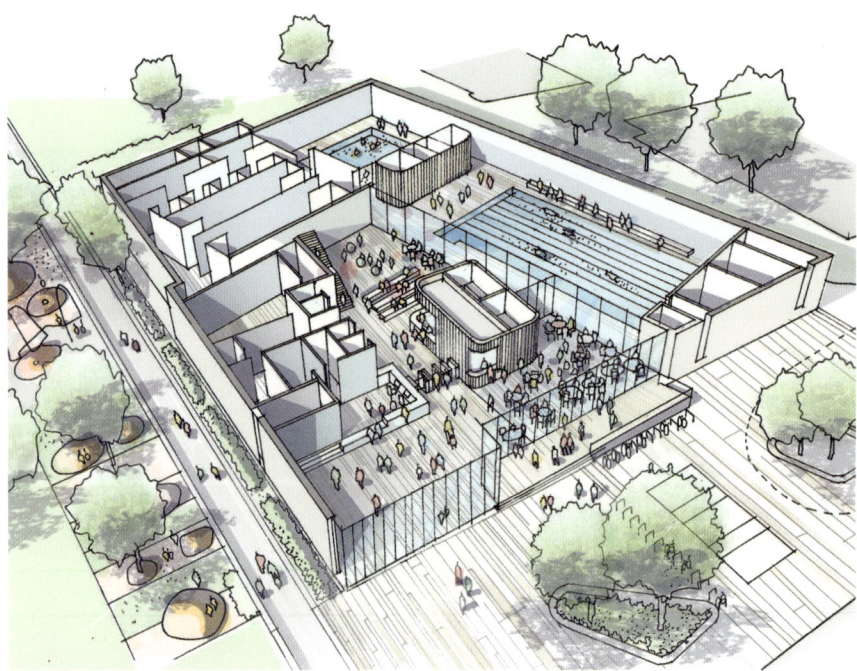

The Castle Centre at Elephant and Castle is the most visited leisure centre in Southwark. It replaced an existing building, ageing and poorly equipped, and focuses on wider issues of health and lifestyle while providing outstanding facilities for swimming, gymnastics, fitness training and dance, together with a creche and café.

Externally the building has an impressive presence, designed as a 'copper box' and making good use of a sloping site. A key aim was to open up views of the activities within to passers-by – potential users. It faces a public space that incorporates the churchyard of the former St Mary's church, with its children's play area. The interior is equally impressive, planned on a 'pinwheel' model – the architects compare the plan to a coiled snake – with the separate elements recognizably independent but coming together in an impressive central courtyard space under a glazed roof. This is a place where people gather, with the café as a social focus, and views into the six-lane, 25-metre swimming pool. From the courtyard, a dramatically formed staircase rises through the building to provide access to the multipurpose studios and sports hall.

The context of the building embraces new high-rise residential buildings and low-rise Victorian housing to the north. It steps up to four storeys where it addresses the tower of One the Elephant (page 60), making a distinctive impact on a dramatically transformed townscape.

The Castle Centre, one element in the radical transformation of Elephant and Castle, provides outstanding facilities for swimming, fitness training and gymnastics, along with a creche and café, and has become hugely popular. In its scale and materials, the building reflects its varied context of old and new.

Culture and Leisure

Mountview

ARCHITECT Turner Works
DATE 2018
ADDRESS 120 Peckham Hill Street, SE15 5JT
CLIENT Mountview

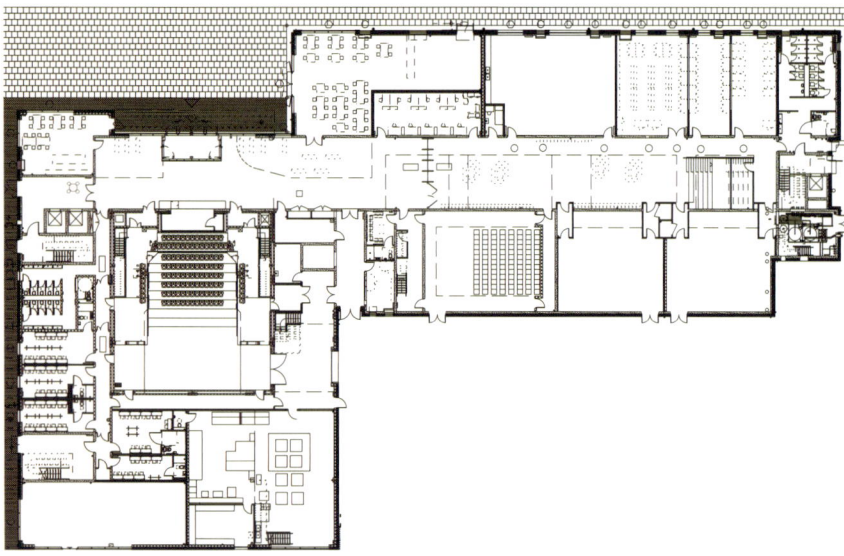

PROPOSED GROUND-FLOOR PLAN

Mountview's new home is in the heart of Peckham, metres from Will Alsop's Stirling Prize-winning public library. Founded in Crouch End in north London in 1945, the academy is recognized as one of Britain's leading drama schools and the alma mater of scores of successful actors. It moved to Peckham after a partnership was forged with Southwark Council, which provided a long-term loan to supplement Mountview's own fundraising campaign.

The location was a brownfield site, previously housing the now defunct Area 10 arts space. The brief was for a building capable of intensive use, housing 400 students and 100 staff, with a fully equipped 200-seat theatre, a set-building workshop and a rooftop restaurant/bar with spectacular views across London. A world-class school for budding performers, this is equally a huge resource for the local community, opening up access to the dramatic arts for local people of all ages in a building that is fully accessible and heavily used.

Turner Works' 10,365-square-metre building is a tough and flexible 'warehouse for the arts'.

At the core of the Corten steel-clad studio block is a naturally lit, full-height central atrium, a place for circulation but equally a meeting space – and sometimes an ad hoc performance space. The adjacent theatre block, clad in black brick, is a vibrant public facility with a regular programme of performances. Studio spaces, used by students during the day, can be hired in the evenings and at weekends, as part of a revenue-generating programme that is vital to the school's funding. Rehearsal spaces, twenty-one in total, are designed with London's theatre sector in mind, and the partnership helps to foster links that have produced a pipeline of opportunities for Mountview graduates.

This project is within Southwark's Creative Enterprise Zone, designated in 2018, which encompasses much of Camberwell and Peckham and aims to encourage the development of new arts activities in the area, embracing the creation of new employment opportunities for local people. Mountview, housed in a building that so strongly expresses the spirit behind the programme, is a landmark in the growth of the creative arts in Southwark.

This tough, flexible building includes a 200-seat theatre, studio and rehearsal spaces, a set-building workshop and a restaurant.

Culture and Leisure

Southwark Town Hall and Theatre Peckham

The former town hall (right), a competent if undistinguished building that was nevertheless a local landmark, was transformed through a process of conversion and extension to provide rooms for students at Goldsmiths, University of London, plus social spaces, studios, a café and a public gallery. The new 200-seat theatre (opposite), striking in form, with its associated rehearsal and dance studios, offers dance and theatre classes to local young people.

The former town hall on Peckham Road is one of a number of municipal buildings in Southwark that have been imaginatively repurposed. Completed in 1934, it was described by Nikolaus Pevsner as 'singularly undistinguished', but it is a local landmark and an important feature of a Conservation Area. Jestico + Whiles was commissioned in 2013 by developer Alumno – a specialist in student housing – to convert and extend the building as accommodation for students at the world-renowned Goldsmiths, University of London.

The conversion of the town hall, with significant interiors retained as common spaces and lounges, formed one element in a project that provides a total of 155 student rooms, largely in an elegantly detailed new building faced in a pale brick that is in keeping with the Portland stone and weathered brick of the town hall. Relieved by subtle variations in fenestration, the elevations of the building have a contemporary elegance that is in tune with the surviving Georgian architecture of the neighbourhood. A sky lounge at roof level, clad in fritted glass with anodized fins, provides a social space as well as a venue for exhibitions of student work. Twelve artists' studios provide workspace for students. At street level, an independently operated public gallery is complemented by a café.

The new Theatre Peckham is an important feature of the project. Designed in association with theatre consultant Charcoalblue, it replaces the former theatre, which occupied a former church hall. The replacement features a 200-seat auditorium, rehearsal space and dance studio, with breakout and foyer spaces opening on to a new public square. The theatre has a striking exterior, clad in reflective, iridescent porcelain tiles and recalling, in its dramatic form, a folded theatre curtain. Theatre Peckham is a venue with a special role in encouraging local youth talent, offering classes in dance, mime and theatre.

New student housing projects have become a feature of inner-city areas in London and provincial cities. This project is distinctive for its positive contribution to the public realm and to the cultural life of Peckham.

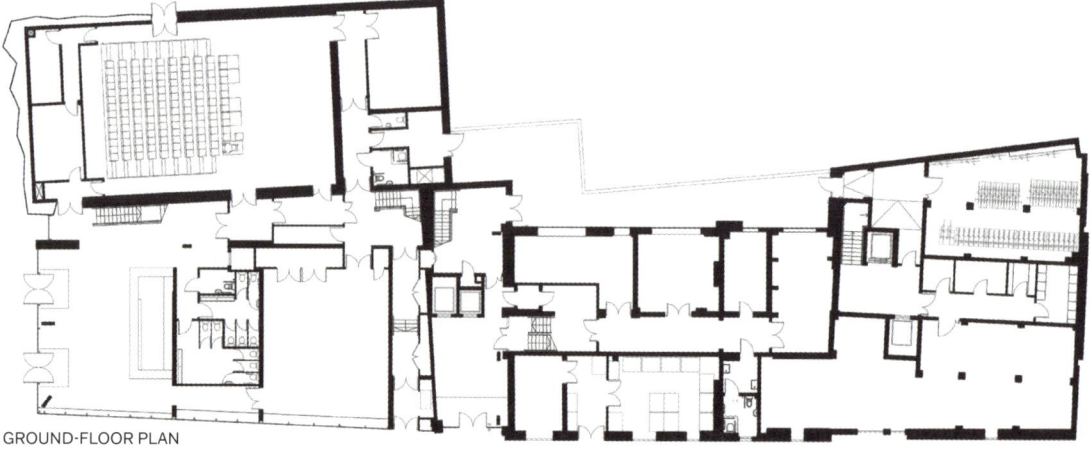

GROUND-FLOOR PLAN

ARCHITECT Jestico + Whiles
DATE 2017
ADDRESS 221 Havil Street, SE5 7SB
CLIENT General Projects

Culture and Leisure

Siobhan Davies Dance Studios

ARCHITECT Sarah Wigglesworth Architects
DATE 2005
ADDRESS 85 St George's Road, SE1 6ER
CLIENT Siobhan Davies Dance Company

Dame Siobhan Davies is one of the leading figures on the British dance scene. She founded her own dance company in 1988, and the studio development completed in 2005 embodies her belief in 'the power of dance for social and artistic change'. Involvement with the local community is fundamental to its work, alongside professional development for established dancers.

The search for a permanent home for her company led Davies to a former school building near Elephant and Castle, an 1890s structure several times extended. The company needed two performance and rehearsal spaces, one capable of accommodating an audience, and the building contained internal spaces that would be ideal. In addition, the brief provided for offices, meeting rooms, and changing and therapy spaces, demanding bold changes to the existing building.

The former school consisted of two blocks separated by a narrow circulation slot, which was stripped out to become a double-height space at the heart of the building. The western block accommodates offices and changing rooms. The eastern block was converted to contain meeting and entertainment spaces, with the smaller of the two performance spaces on the first floor. The main performance studio could not be accommodated within the existing building. A striking space 5 metres high, it sits at roof level, its dramatic timber-arched structure twisting to support a billowing GRP (glass-reinforced plastic) roof that Sarah Wigglesworth has memorably compared to a loaf of bread rising from a baking tin. Suffused with controlled daylight, the studio is an inspiring space, almost baroque in its spatial drama. Wigglesworth compares the experience of using it to dancing on the roof.

NORTH ELEVATION

EAST ELEVATION

The project provides meeting and therapy rooms and a variety of performance spaces, the most dramatic of them a timber-arched top-floor studio roofed in glass-reinforced plastic.

Culture and Leisure

Southwark Park Pavilion

ARCHITECT Bell Phillips
DATE 2019
ADDRESS Access via Gomm Road, SE16 2ET
CLIENT London Borough of Southwark

Southwark Park, which opened in 1869, is one of the major open spaces in south London, 25 hectares in extent, a vital green lung complete with lake, bowling green, tennis courts, cricket pitch, children's play area, art gallery and a highly rated public café. It was the subject of a refurbishment project funded by the National Lottery Heritage Fund and completed in 2001, and this has reinforced its status as a major public amenity.

The site for the pavilion, in accord with a masterplan by Kinnear Landscape Architects, is in a pivotal position, overlooking the boating lake. Envisaged as a classic parkland pavilion, a twenty-first-century restatement of a Georgian model, it brings together a number of facilities – café, park offices and public conveniences – under one roof.

The striking tripartite plan of the building is a response to the context of the surrounding landscape, so that its three elevations address different elements in the park (the lake to the west, the cricket field to the southeast and the art gallery to the northeast) and provide triple-aspect views. A broad terrace by the lake provides spill-out space for the café. The white brick façades form a cool contrast to the surrounding green landscape. The extended

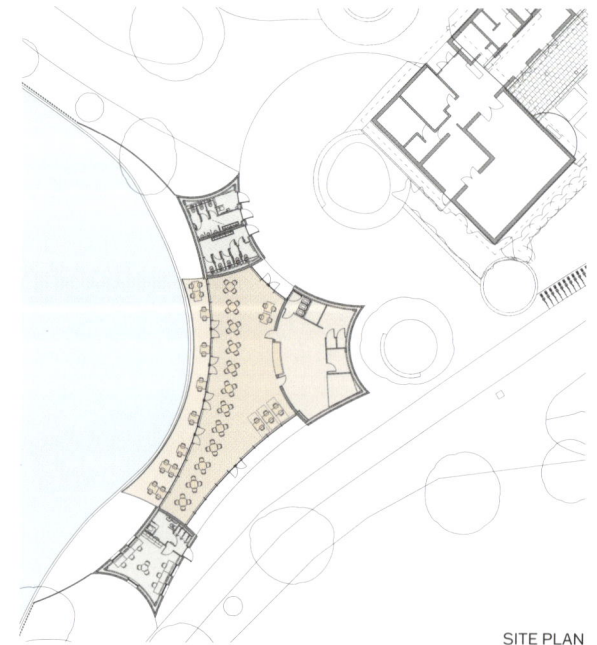

SITE PLAN

Culture and Leisure

façade to the lake is cut away, with a panoramic strip of glazing capitalizing on the view.

In its aesthetic a minimalist structure, free of extraneous gestures – indeed, strikingly functional – the building is equally a response to the landscape in the tradition of the long-lost pavilions and grottoes of the Georgian Vauxhall Pleasure Gardens, reconsidered for a more democratic age.

The renovation of Southwark Park included the restoration of the boating lake (above). Bell Phillips' building is a twenty-first-century version of the pavilions that were a key feature of Georgian pleasure gardens. Its minimalist design responds to the green landscape that surrounds it.

Culture and Leisure

Blavatnik Building
Tate Modern

ARCHITECT Herzog & de Meuron
DATE 2016
ADDRESS Holland Street/Sumner Street, SE1 9TG
CLIENT Tate

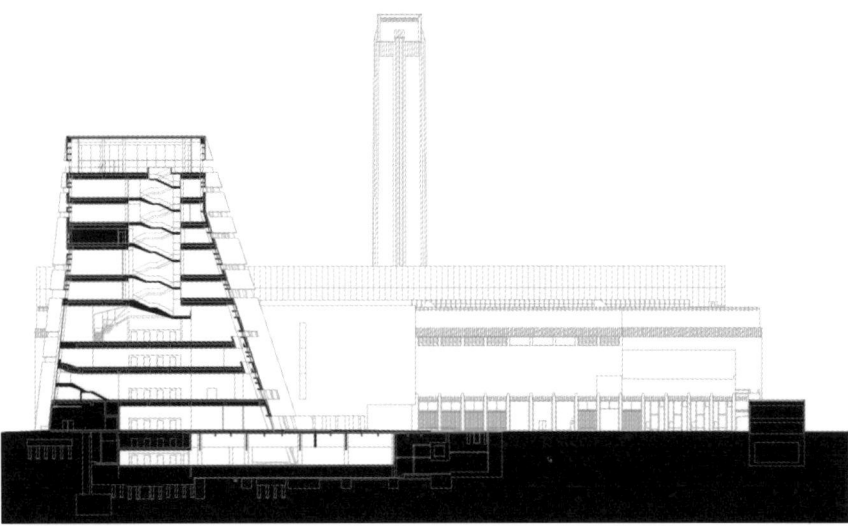

SECTION

SITE PLAN

Bankside power station, occupying a prominent site on the south bank of the River Thames, facing St Paul's Cathedral, was constructed between 1947 and 1963. As at the earlier Battersea power station, Giles Gilbert Scott was called in to give the building architectural form. Bankside closed in 1981, its future the subject of much debate before it was identified as the home for the Tate gallery's modern and contemporary collections. Herzog & de Meuron's transformation of the building into Tate Modern was completed in 2000.

A section at the rear of the building remained in operational use until 2000. In 2007 Herzog & de Meuron was commissioned to design a major extension, initially known as the Switch House but renamed after a major donation from the businessman and philanthropist Sir Leonard Blavatnik.

The building, decisively opening a new gateway to Tate Modern from the south, sits on the power station's former oil tanks, which have been converted into dramatic display spaces, their interiors left as raw concrete. It is anything but a contextual addition; rising to 64.5 metres and containing eleven levels, it can be seen clearly from across the Thames, a rival to the retained landmark chimney that is a defining element of the converted building.

The first designs for this major addition – with an area of 23,000 square metres – envisaged it as a series of glass boxes stacked in asymmetrical form: striking, yet anything but contextual. A redesign retained the basic form of the building as a ziggurat rising from a trapezoidal base, but brick replaced glass as the exterior cladding, with the bricks bonded in advance and laid in a staggered pattern to allow controlled natural light to permeate the interior. The choice of material ensures a visual connection with the former power station, but contrasts with the context of new commercial and residential buildings, including RSHP's Neo Bankside (page 56), yards away.

The Blavatnik Building provides not only more gallery spaces but also education and meeting rooms and a rooftop restaurant. Its structure is exposed internally to dramatic

The Blavatnik Building is a typically radical project by Herzog & de Meuron, contextual only in its use of brick cladding in deference to Giles Gilbert Scott's former power station. The ziggurat-like form of the building makes it a landmark, challenging the dominance of Scott's chimney.

effect, with sculptural stairs forming a memorable route for visitors. The earlier conversion of the power station, for all its heroic scale, offered only one memorable interior, in the form of the great turbine hall. But with the extension Herzog & de Meuron had the opportunity to design a new building that displays to the full their ability to create strikingly innovative form.

Culture and Leisure

Una Marson Library

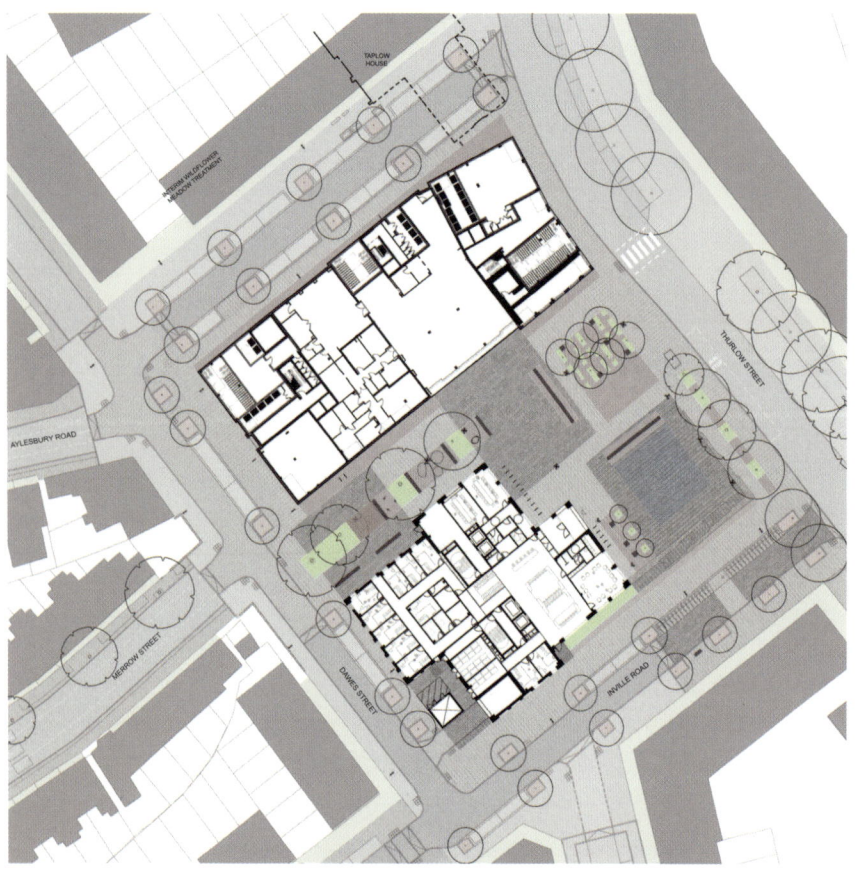

The Una Marson Library, one element in the comprehensive renewal of the Aylesbury estate in Walworth, is named in honour of the Jamaican activist and writer Una Marson (1905–1965). Marson spent the years of the Second World War as an influential broadcaster in London, living for a time in Brunswick Square, Camberwell, and was the first Black woman to work at the BBC.

The library, which occupies the ground floor of a residential block addressing a public square on a new pedestrian route leading from Dawes Street to Thurlow Street, is much more than a place for reading. Described as 'a haven for the community', it contains a 110-square-metre community space, plus two meeting rooms divided by a sliding partition. The building, part of an ambitious programme of investment in public libraries by Southwark Council – six new libraries have opened since 2010 – is designed as a flexible amenity for the neighbourhood. The library proper, which includes a designated children's space, features a strikingly dynamic fire-resistant ceiling formed of timber ribs in an articulated diamond pattern, almost Gothic in its effect. The interior is colourful, light and welcoming, an inspirational space named after an inspirational woman.

ARCHITECT HTA Design
DATE 2024
ADDRESS 62 Thurlow Street, SE17 2GB
CLIENT London Borough of Southwark

The library is a resource for the whole community. It contains not only books and periodicals – and a children's section – but also work and study spaces offering the free use of PCs, and a large public hall and meeting rooms.

Housing

Slum clearance and the impact of wartime bombing made housing an urgent issue in Southwark after 1945. The failure, in terms of social as well as physical fabric, of some major housing schemes has launched a massive campaign of reconstruction, with the redevelopment of the Aylesbury and Heygate estates. The provision of new housing, reflecting the social transformation of Southwark in recent decades, has been undertaken by the local authority, private developers and housing trusts. In Bermondsey, the London Square development is providing new affordable/social housing (35 per cent of the total on the site) on reclaimed industrial land. While prestigious new private residential projects – for example Two Fifty One, close to Elephant and Castle, and One Blackfriars, close to Blackfriars Bridge – have been largely high-rise, remaking Southwark's skyline, housing associations and trusts have built projects that are more clearly contextual. Examples are Panter Hudspith's Royal Road, where 80 per cent of homes are rented, and Haworth Tompkins' Stead Street development.

'Such a wonderful space, so much to do, so much community spirit. A complete success story.'

A RELATIVE OF AN APPLEBY BLUE RESIDENT

95 Peckham Road

ARCHITECT Peter Barber Architects
DATE 2019
ADDRESS 95 Peckham Road, SE15 5FA
CLIENT Kuropatwa Ltd

AXONOMETRIC

GROUND-FLOOR PLAN

Described as 'the miracle creator of dazzling streets', Peter Barber has been responsible for a series of housing projects across London that reflect his remarkable ability as a maker of memorable form and his willingness to revisit and reinvent traditional forms. The development at Peckham Road is an example of his approach. The site is alongside a heavily trafficked road, but Barber places most of the new homes in a block that boldly addresses the street and breaks with the monotonous regularity typified in so many recent housing developments in London. The substantial bulk of the building, ziggurat-like, faced in pale brick and stepping back from the road, provides a memory of the mansion blocks of the late Victorian and Edwardian periods.

But Barber's architecture, while respectful of historic precedents, addresses the needs of twenty-first-century society. This six-storey building of 2,846 square metres, with a total of thirty-three homes, contains a mix of flats and two-storey maisonettes. (There are more maisonettes around a communal courtyard to the rear, a space that was designed to be used by the residents of the whole development.) The units are accessed via doors opening on to the street, leading into tiny private courtyard gardens. On every upper level balconies and generous roof terraces – a far remove from the tiny external spaces of a traditional tenement block – are a social amenity, but equally serve to break up the perceived mass of the building. The architect anticipated that these spaces would be filled with plants, garden seats and umbrellas, and the building was designed to be taken over as the territory of its residents, enriched not despoiled.

The roadside, south-facing site of the development made effective insulation vital, and a mechanical heat-recovery ventilation system is an amenity in warm weather. The development's progressive energy agenda is in tune with the social ambitions of a project that seeks to reinvent the mansion block for a new age and a new society.

The project is a good example of Peter Barber's approach to urban housing, with the scale of a traditional London mansion block but incorporating generous balconies, roof terraces and courtyard gardens. Beautifully crafted in pale brick, the building fronts a busy street.

Housing

Albion Street Housing

ARCHITECT Bell Phillips
ADDRESS Albion Street, SE16 7JQ
DATE 2024
CLIENT London Borough of Southwark

ELEVATION

The site for this residential development in Rotherhithe, with twenty-six homes for social and intermediate rent, was formerly occupied by a 1960s civic centre designed by the architectural practice YRM and demolished in 2016. (The public library it incorporated became redundant following the opening of the nearby Canada Water Library; page 20.) Close to the Rotherhithe Tunnel, the site was bookended by two listed buildings, the 1950s Finnish Seamen's Church (also designed by YRM) and the 1920s St Olave's church, a mission to Norwegian seamen. But a major element in the context was housing of mid- to late-twentieth-century vintage, constructed in the wake of wartime bomb damage. Bell Phillips' design sought to respond to the potent presence of the two churches, one low-key neo-Georgian in style, the other strikingly modernist, its use of contrasting red-and-white brick and square punched windows echoing the language of the Finnish church.

The brief for the development included the provision of an upgraded public square, designed to cater for popular local markets, and flexible retail/community space at ground-floor level. It contains a range of one-, two- and three-bedroom flats designed to cater for different household needs. The shallow depth of the building allows most of the units to be double-aspect, with excellent thermal comfort,

ventilation and natural light. Living rooms are set at the north of the plan to minimize interference from traffic noise. Most of the flats are dual-aspect and all have private balconies overlooking the public square and inset within a scalloped façade to combine privacy with visual interest. The building steps back at the fourth floor, where a roof terrace is provided for the use of all residents.

Occupying a site between two listed churches, this project is respectful in scale, its architectural language making subtle reference to that of its neighbours. The new housing is designed to cope with the proximity of a busy road. A significant benefit of the scheme is the provision of a new public square (above).

Housing

Appleby Blue

ARCHITECT Witherford Watson Mann Architects
DATE 2023
ADDRESS 94–116 Southwark Park Road, SE16 3RD
CLIENT United St Saviour's Charity

The almshouse, a building type with a long history, is traditionally a retreat from the world, a place for the elderly to live out their last years. Hiram's Hospital, imagined by Anthony Trollope in his novel *Barchester Towers* (1857), offered the image of a paternalistic, controlled environment, a semi-monastic sanctuary apart from the world. Appleby Blue reinvents the almshouse for a new age.

Commissioned by United St Saviour's Charity, an organization with its roots in the sixteenth century, the development, on the site of an (abandoned) former care home and car park, houses some sixty-three residents over the age of sixty-five. On a busy high street in the heart of Bermondsey, with a bus stop outside, it is seen as a place where residents can live an active life and be part of the local community rather than be shut away.

At its heart is the Garden Court designed by Grant Associates, a lush space 40 metres long with a fountain feeding a stream that flows among trees and woodland flowers. A tranquil retreat, it is enjoyed by residents and their visitors. Gardens are a fundamental ingredient in the project. A roof garden at second-floor level contains raised beds for fruit, herbs and vegetables, and is maintained by the residents with help from local volunteers.

Positioned between the Garden Court and the street, the double-height Garden Room is a space not only for residents but equally for the local community. A fully equipped community kitchen with regular events further cements links with the neighbourhood, with the aim of bridging the traditional gulf between residents and local people. Some of the food is grown onsite. A library and a hobby and skills room encourage residents to remain active – and perhaps improve their IT skills. The architecture of the project is itself welcoming and humane – with big, timber-framed windows to the street and warm brick above.

The residents' flats – single-bedroom units of 55 square metres and doubles of 79 square metres – are arranged around the Garden Court, limited to two storeys on the south side to allow unimpeded sunlight to permeate the court. All flats are dual-aspect, and are accessed from a glazed gallery overlooking the Garden Court. This is a place to socialize, with sliding windows that can be thrown open in fine weather, a cordial alternative to private balconies. The whole development is passively ventilated, and more than a third of the energy required to run it is generated from solar panels installed on the roof.

This development on a busy high street constitutes a reinvention of the traditional almshouse, with its monastic associations. It is set around a communal garden, and plots on the roof provide fruit and vegetables for the residents. A community kitchen, library and IT room encourage residents to pursue an active life. There is nothing monastic about the architecture of this finely crafted building.

Housing

Chapter London Bridge

ARCHITECT KPF
DATE 2025
ADDRESS 40–46 Weston Street, SE1 3QD
CLIENT Greystar

London is a world centre of higher education, attracting students from across the globe. The site for KPF's Chapter development, containing 905 student rooms, is next to the Guy's campus of King's College (founded 1829) and to London Bridge station. It replaces a nondescript 1960s office building.

The thirty-nine-storey building, 138 metres high, addresses a very varied context. It is close to the Bermondsey Conservation Area, but equally has as a near neighbour the Shard (page 104). It stands in a dynamic area of new development with a long history – Southwark Cathedral and Borough Market are nearby. The base of the building is deliberately contextual, relating to and interacting with the street but set back behind a colonnade, which allows a widened pavement. It contains shops, meeting rooms and amenity spaces. The use of terracotta cladding draws on the language of nearby warehouses.

By contrast the tower 'interacts with the sky', in the words of its designer, drawing inspiration in its folded form from the art of origami. It appears to change as one moves around the building – radically different from the smooth regularity of the Shard, reflecting its residential use. The accommodation provided in the building reflects a variety of student lifestyles by including self-contained studios and clusters of two or three bedrooms with shared facilities. In common with other high-quality student housing projects, cafés, a gym and a cinema are included in the development, along with a striking terrace at level 37.

Chapter is a thirty-nine-storey student village, a response to the growth of higher education in London. The building's folded façade makes it a distinctive presence on the skyline, and the base of the tower contains shops and other amenities for residents.

LEVEL 4 PLAN

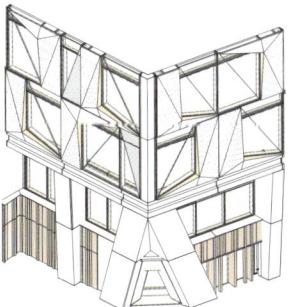

ORIGAMI AXONOMETRIC

Housing

Aylesbury Estate Block SO1 and Harriet Hardy Extra Care

The Aylesbury housing estate in Walworth, with more than 2,700 units, was constructed in 1963–77. It was a heroic achievement, but one that eventually declined in both physical and social terms, leading to Southwark's not uncontroversial decision in 2005 to demolish and rebuild the whole estate. The first phase of new development consists of six blocks of housing – four by HTA Design and one each from Hawkins\Brown and Mae – in a masterplan by HTA.

Mae's Block SO1 at the southwestern end of the site provides 119 new homes, all for rent and with special provision for older residents with special care needs. It includes a community centre on the ground floor containing a central room seating 100 and

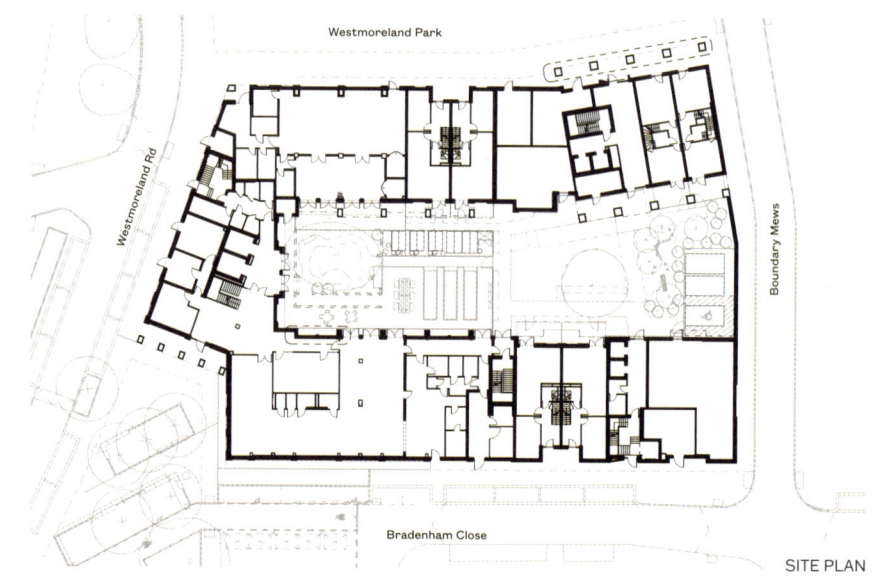

SITE PLAN

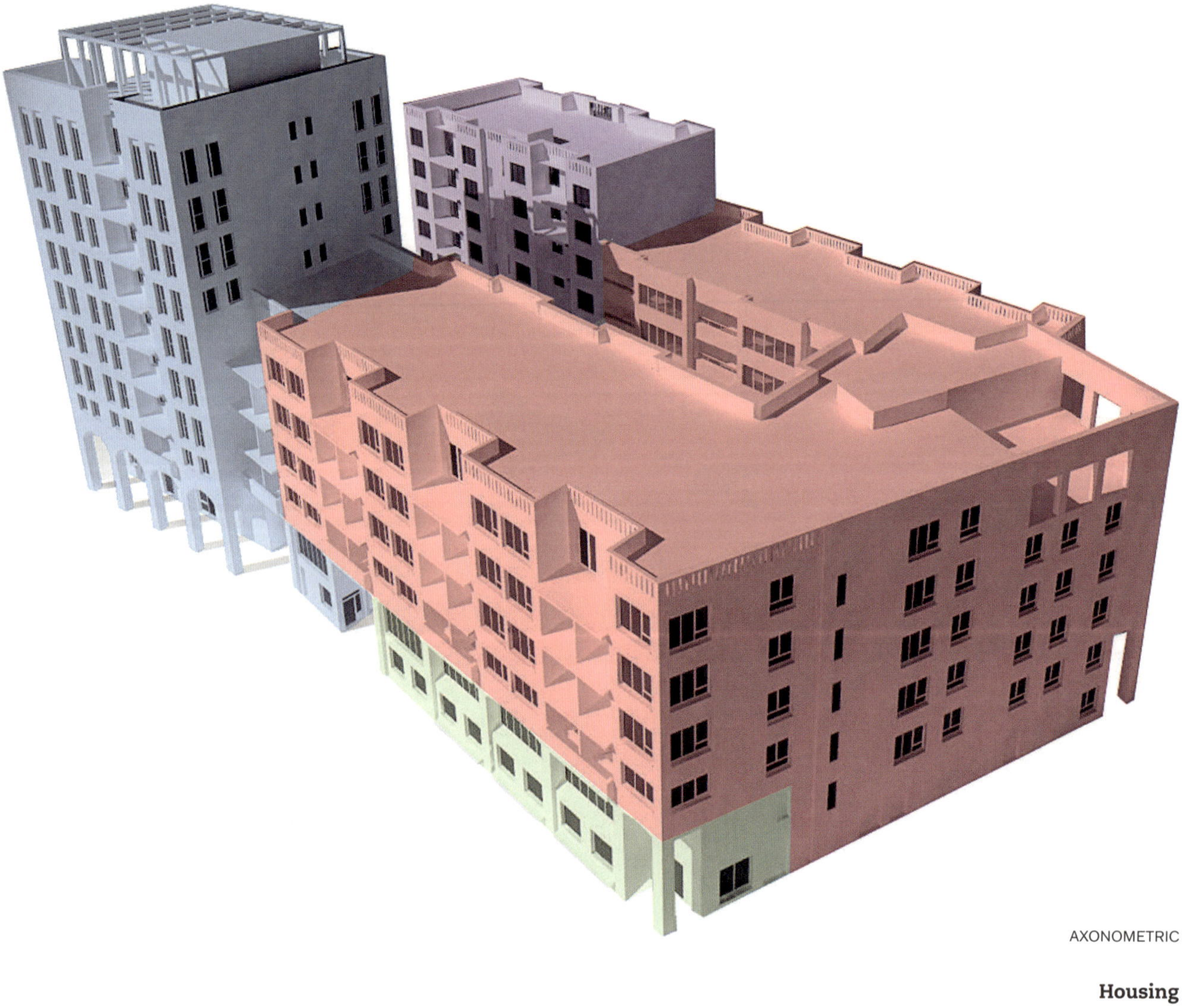

AXONOMETRIC

Housing

ARCHITECTS HTA Design | Mae
DATE 2023
ADDRESS Westmoreland Road, SE17 2AY
CLIENT London Borough of Southwark

The strong façades and brick colonnades offer a sense of grandeur and a warmer aesthetic than the concrete housing blocks they replaced.

Housing

two smaller rooms that can be opened up to create a larger space. The scheme is clad in warm brick, its aesthetic far removed from the bare concrete of the demolished estate. Its strongly articulated façades, with a brick colonnade at ground level, found inspiration, the architect reports, from John Soane's nearby church of St Peter.

At each end of the U-shaped development is general-needs housing for individuals, couples and families (in units of one to four bedrooms), rising to a maximum of ten storeys. Two-storey town houses for families form the base of the block. The landscaped courtyard at the heart of the project is an amenity for residents, with retained mature trees and raised beds for flowers and vegetables. Double-height arches mark the point of entry.

SECTION

The Harriet Hardy Extra Care Centre contains fifty-four flats for older people. The scheme is, perhaps, unusual in locating care facilities, including units designed for disabled people, within a larger housing block. This is a distinct move towards integrating the elderly into society.

Occupying the central part of the development, it is conceived as a new species of almshouse, designed for the twenty-first century and conceived around the idea of progressive privacy. It provides independent living for residents, housed in flats over six storeys, accessed from short corridors leading from indoor/outdoor decks looking into the communal garden. The decks are wide enough to encourage residents to sit out, socialize and feel part of a community.

The flats are generous in size, with an open-plan layout that facilitates easy movement for their occupants, including wheelchair users. Balconies and low window ledges overlook a garden designed for residents and a public space to east and west. On the ground floor, addressing the street, a communal lounge, kitchen and dining room are arranged as connecting spaces that can be thrown together for social events, part of a theme of flexibility and adaptability that characterizes the scheme.

Arranged around a courtyard garden, Harriet Hardy Extra Care is an almshouse for the twenty-first century, with excellent provision for disabled people, communal eating and socializing spaces, and generously scaled flats.

Housing

London Square

ARCHITECT Allford Hall Monaghan Morris | Coffey Architects
DATE 2025
ADDRESS Grange Road, SE1 3BH
CLIENT London Square Developments Ltd

The site of the London Square development was the run-down Rich industrial estate near Old Kent Road in Bermondsey. It retained several significant, although unlisted, buildings associated with the food-processing and tanning industries that were once major employers.

These buildings had been adapted in recent decades to house two resident arts organizations, Tannery Arts and Southwark Studios. Their retention was an important element in the masterplan developed by Allford Hall Monaghan Morris (AHMM), which provided for commercial, residential and retail development – more than 400 new homes, 35 per cent of them affordable/social, with a 20,000-square-metre commercial hub dedicated to small and medium-sized businesses – in line with the objectives of Southwark Council's Old Kent Road Opportunity Area. AHMM's masterplan retains the warehouses, carefully inserting new architecture to create generous courtyards and tight alleys reminiscent of the Bermondsey of old.

AERIAL VIEW

Existing buildings that housed vanished local industries have been retained and converted as part of a masterplan that respects the history of the area.

Housing

Housing 51

Coffey Architects, appointed after a competition, completed a significant element of the London Square project in 2023, combining conversion and restoration with new-build. Three buildings – a new residential structure, a warehouse mixed-use conversion and a new gallery, studio and educational space for Tannery Arts – are set around a landscaped courtyard. The retained warehouse building is capped with two new storeys of residential space, while the lower floors contain studios.

The Tannery residential building, dubbed 'the bar of light', contains four storeys of dual-aspect flats, clad in a screen of white aluminium, set above two brick-clad lower floors containing town houses and entered via a dramatic black concrete staircase.

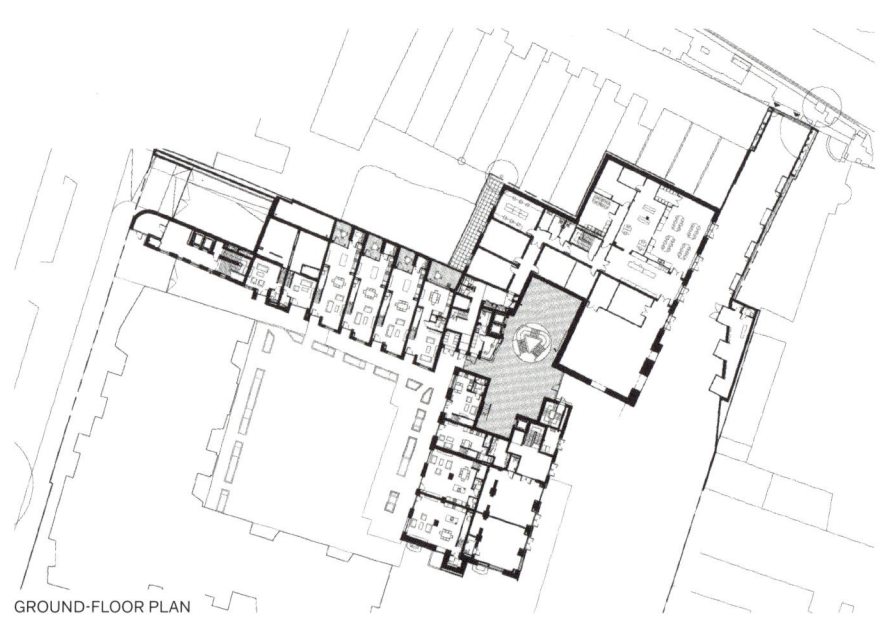

GROUND-FLOOR PLAN

Coffey Architects' project within the London Square development is a mix of existing and new, providing new housing, as well as space for arts organizations long based on the site.

The architecture of the various new buildings references the historic context, with the use of simple brickwork. The rhythm of the façades is enhanced by the deep loggias. Retained warehouses were adapted and extended in a complementary manner, the scars of history celebrated rather than erased. The final phase, replacing a mundane industrial shed of recent date on the southwestern corner of the site, includes three residential buildings around a landscaped courtyard, again designed by AHMM.

A key ingredient of the entire project – to be completed fully in 2026 – is the landscaping strategy, with green spaces renewing land contaminated by centuries of industrial use. Public and private gardens have been created, each responding to its architectural context, and more than 100 trees planted. New pedestrian routes thread past gardens and commercial frontages, connecting the new mixed-use quarter with surrounding streets.

Manor Place Housing

ARCHITECT Pollard Thomas Edwards
DATE 2020
ADDRESS Manor Place, SE17 3BD
CLIENT Notting Hill Genesis

The public baths and wash-house complex at Manor Place is a relic of Victorian philanthropy. Opened in 1895 to designs by the architect Edward I'Anson, it was closed in 1978 following the demolition of most of the surrounding housing, and parts of the complex were subsequently demolished. Listed Grade II in 1996, the surviving buildings found a temporary use as a Buddhist centre and in 2013, already vacant, were acquired by Notting Hill Genesis housing association, along with neighbouring land used as a recycling depot and owned by Southwark Council. These elements were incorporated into a housing scheme providing 270 new homes of mixed tenure, exemplifying the aims of Southwark's Elephant and Castle Opportunity Area, of which the site is part.

The listed baths and the adjacent railway arches, carrying a line that bisects the site, became key elements in a development project that has created a new neighbourhood within a short walk of two Underground stations, and with generous public spaces woven through it.

SITE PLAN

The new neighbourhood includes a listed Victorian public bathhouse, converted to residential and small business accommodation.

Most of the undistinguished buildings on the site were demolished, while the former coroner's court and part of the baths complex were converted to residential use. The court building, although unlisted, was retained in response to the views of local residents, and now forms a distinctive addition to the area. Most of the new residential accommodation, which consists of one- to three-bedroom units providing market, intermediate and affordable rent accommodation, is in new blocks up to seven storeys in height. The railway arches were converted to commercial use, with further space in the former baths and wash house for small businesses focusing on the creative industries.

The architectural language of the project responds to and respects the existing context, with several varieties of brick as the predominant material for the new buildings. The landscaping strategy includes generous play areas, as well as pedestrian and cycle routes that form part of Southwark's 'low line' link to the river.

Housing

Neo Bankside

ARCHITECT RSHP
DATE 2012
ADDRESS Holland Street, SE1 9NX
CLIENT Native Land

Neo Bankside is a development that employs an architectural language typical of RSHP – and of the practice of Richard Rogers, from which it sprang. Located immediately to the south of Tate Modern (page 32), it contains a total of 217 flats in 5 blocks, hexagonal in form, ranging from 12 to 24 storeys, providing a total of 28,600 square metres of accommodation.

The flats vary in size from one-bed studios to penthouses with four bedrooms expressed as independent pavilion structures with double-height living areas. Winter gardens at the north and south ends of each building are expressed as prows, suspended from

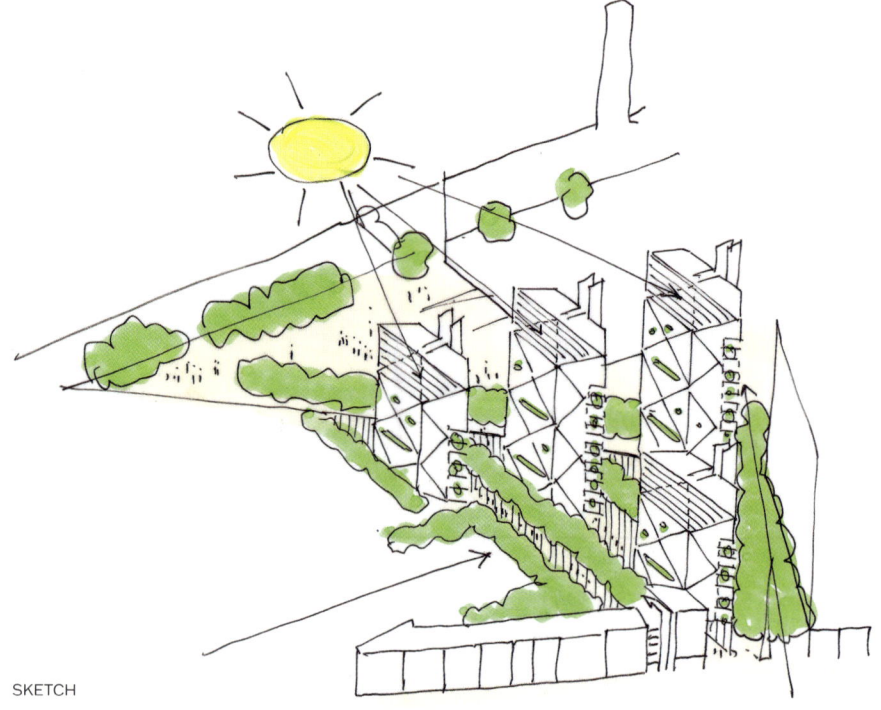

SKETCH

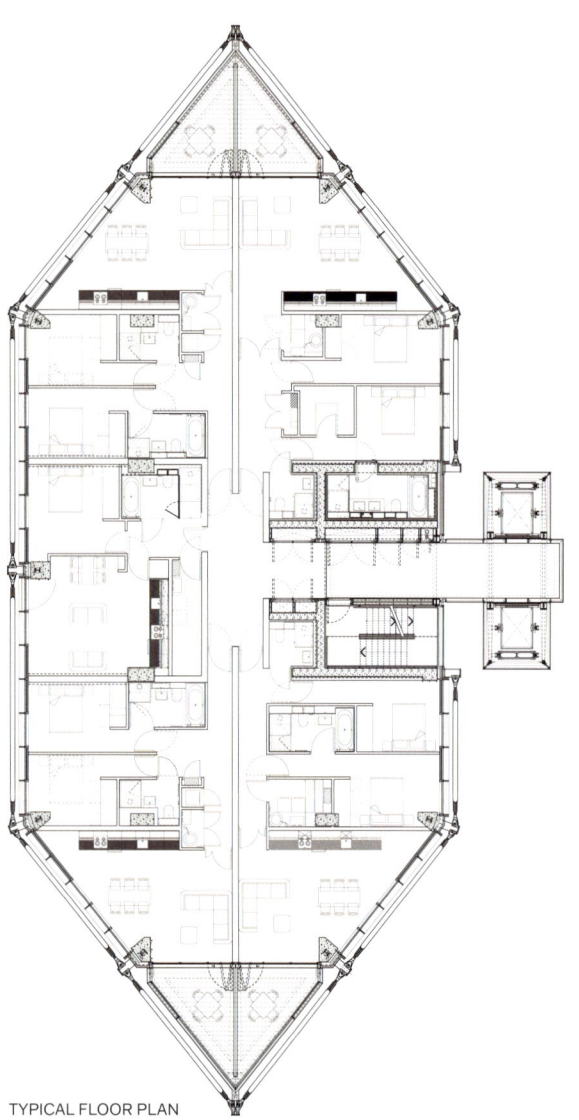

TYPICAL FLOOR PLAN

the main structure on a lightweight deck, addressing neighbouring streets. Access to the flats is provided via glazed lift towers, offering impressive views of the city. There are shops at ground level, and the landscaping around the buildings provides new public routes from Tate Modern to Southwark Street.

The context of the project is varied. The massive scale of the former power station contrasts with that of the modest eighteenth-century Hopton's Almshouses, while Southwark Street contains a mix of Victorian and later buildings, varied in scale.

The architecture of Neo Bankside is colourful, expressive, carefully detailed and in tune with the industrial heritage of the South Bank. The external diagrid bracing, a familiar feature of the practice's work, is a fundamental element, allowing internal structural walls to be dispensed with to create highly flexible spaces. In a dense urban setting, privacy was a key consideration – proximity to Tate Modern was one issue – and louvred timber screens set between the panels of the double glazing address this, as well as providing protection from solar heat gain.

The architecture is in the best Richard Rogers tradition, with a clear expression of structure and a bold use of colour.

Housing 57

One Blackfriars

ARCHITECT SimpsonHaugh
DATE 2019
ADDRESS Blackfriars Road, SE1 9GD
CLIENT St George

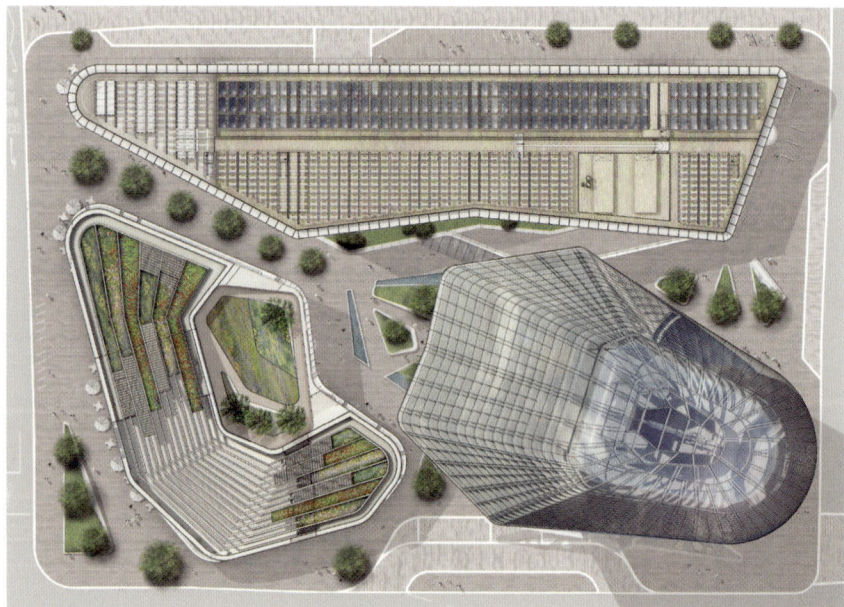
GROUND AND ROOF PLAN

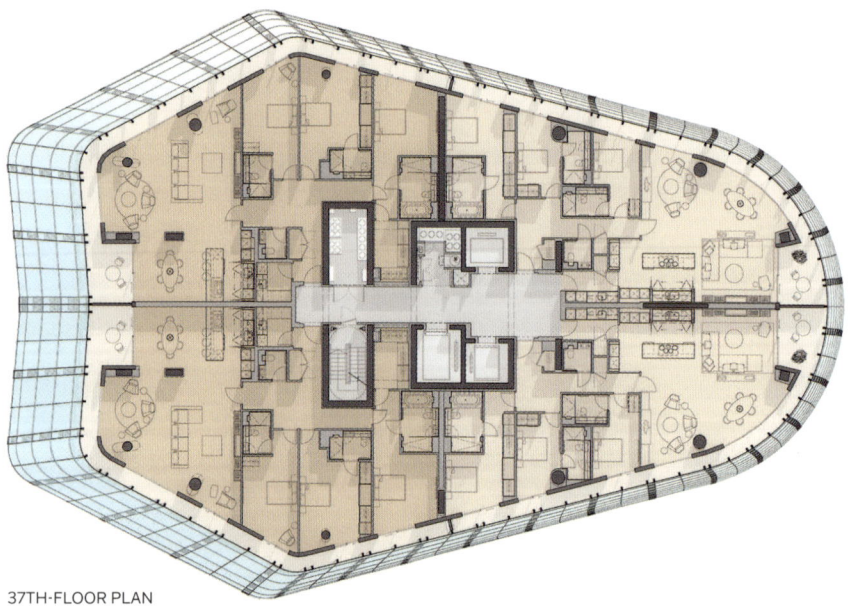
37TH-FLOOR PLAN

The fifty-storey, 170-metre One Blackfriars tower is unquestionably a new landmark in Southwark. Given planning permission by Southwark Council in 2012, the project was the successor to a proposed 225-metre tower of sixty-eight storeys, the planning application for which was withdrawn after objections to its impact on the London skyline. The striking form of the new tower, which stands on the southern approach to Blackfriars Bridge and contains 274 flats, has led to its being nicknamed 'the Boomerang'.

A previous application for a tower on the site, approved by Southwark Council in 2007, was called in to a public inquiry in 2008 and subsequently approved by the then Secretary of State, despite objections from neighbouring local authorities and from English Heritage. Ownership of the site changed in 2011, with planning permission renewed and developer St George progressing the scheme. Construction began in 2013.

The tower is the central element in a project that also features a podium building containing shops, restaurants and a swimming pool, spa and cinema for the use of residents, and a separate block housing the 161-bed Bankside Hotel. A public piazza forms a focus for the development.

The tower is clad in an innovative double façade. The outer skin is made up of 5,476 curved glass panels, while the inner skin is formed of coloured glass panels, which change in hue from dark to light as they ascend. The space between the two layers is deep enough to house winter gardens and generous private balconies for residents, and is naturally ventilated via powered louvres.

A dominant element on the riverside at Blackfriars Bridge, the carefully considered form of One Blackfriars makes it a new London landmark. A separate block contains a hotel, and the new square is usable by all.

Housing

One the Elephant

ARCHITECT Squire & Partners
DATE 2016
ADDRESS 1 St Gabriel Walk, SE1 6FA
CLIENT Lendlease

This thirty-seven-storey apartment building is one element of a masterplan by Squire & Partners, commissioned by developer Lendlease for a site that forms part of Southwark's comprehensive £2.3 billion regeneration project for Elephant and Castle. In addition to this landmark residential tower, a four-storey pavilion block providing retail and community space, as well as flats, mediates between the new development and the Grade II-listed Metropolitan Tabernacle, a survivor from the Victorian era. The third element of the masterplan is the leisure centre designed by John McAslan + Partners (page 22). The new buildings sit in a landscaped setting, offering pedestrian routes in an area long dominated by road traffic and connecting to a playground area designed by the landscape architect and educator Martha Schwartz.

The slender tower contains 284 flats, plus leisure and retail space. A generous reception area provides access to the building, which is designed to house a new city community. Each flat has its own balcony, offering views across London, and there is a spacious lounge area for the use of all residents, suitable for a wide range of events from private dinners to children's parties. The lounge, along with reception areas, hallways and lift lobbies, was styled by the architects. The artist Robin Duttson and Maria Cheung of Squire & Partners were responsible for a programme of artworks themed on the history of Elephant and Castle, recalling the time when it was the centre of a network of market gardens and orchards.

The exteriors of the residential buildings share a materials palette of stone, glass and metallized panels. A special feature of the project is the extensive use of planting, ranging from a moss wall in the reception area to a residents' garden and allotments on the roof of the pavilion block. Environmentally progressive, this development sets a marker for the ongoing regeneration of Elephant and Castle.

SITE PLAN

Flanked by a new leisure centre and by the listed Metropolitan Tabernacle, the residential tower, set in a landscaped area, is a key part of the area's renewal. A subsidiary four-storey block contains retail and community space.

Royal Road Housing

ARCHITECT Panter Hudspith Architects
DATE 2013
ADDRESS Royal Road/Otto Street, SE17 3DA
CLIENT Affinity Sutton Homes

The demolition of the Heygate estate at Elephant and Castle, with the loss of 1,200 homes, generated an urgent need for a strategy to rehouse displaced residents, adding to an existing need for affordable accommodation in the borough. Panter Hudspith Architects' Royal Road project was one of a number of Early Housing Sites commissioned by the council (the first, designed by dRMM, was completed in 2006).

Royal Road, developed in partnership with Affinity Sutton Homes, provides ninety-six affordable homes – 80 per cent of them rented, the remainder under shared ownership – on a site previously occupied by a day centre for the elderly and surrounded by mature trees. The imperative to retain the trees was a prime generator of the site plan, which focuses on a central courtyard and play area and pulls the housing blocks, four to nine storeys in height, back from the surrounding streets. In contrast to the other schemes developed under the Early Housing Sites programme, where lightweight cladding systems were generally used, Royal Road is clad in brick on an in-situ concrete frame, echoing the character of the surrounding area. Two types of brick were selected for their soft and varied tones, and reconstituted stone forms a ground-floor plinth that extends into garden walls. Homes on the ground floor have small private gardens, while others have balconies or access to roof terraces.

In other respects, the scheme set a high standard for 'social' housing. The flats – most of which are triple-aspect with generous natural light – exceed minimum space standards by up to 20 per cent. Access by stairs and lifts to each block avoids the use of depressing internal corridors. The two upper floors step back to provide roof terraces serving two-storey family homes, an element in the carefully considered massing that responds to the diversity of scale in the neighbourhood.

Clad in brick in deference to its context, and laid out around a generous central courtyard, the development sets a high mark for new social housing projects.

ELEVATION

Stead Street Housing

ARCHITECT Haworth Tompkins
DATE 2017
ADDRESS Stead Street, SE17 1BP
CLIENT Guinness Partnership

Haworth Tompkins' Stead Street housing occupies a constrained site previously used as a car park, near the junction of Stead Street and Rodney Road. Peabody Trust's Walworth estate, completed in 1914, is a near neighbour. To achieve permeability, the sixty-three social-rent homes in the scheme are contained in three blocks separated by pedestrian routes that provide access to and views of Nursery Row Park, a highly valued local amenity that is currently the subject of an improvement scheme promoted by Southwark Council. The blocks are subdivided to open them up to natural light and views out, and all flats have a dual aspect and balconies.

The three blocks increase in height from four to six storeys on Rodney Road, with the roof forms carefully handled to respond to context and add visual interest, creating an eventful street frontage. The development contains flats providing from one to four bedrooms, with open-access deck gallery circulation and semi-private landscaped courtyards at ground level. A new hall for the neighbouring Church of the English Martyrs was provided as part of the development.

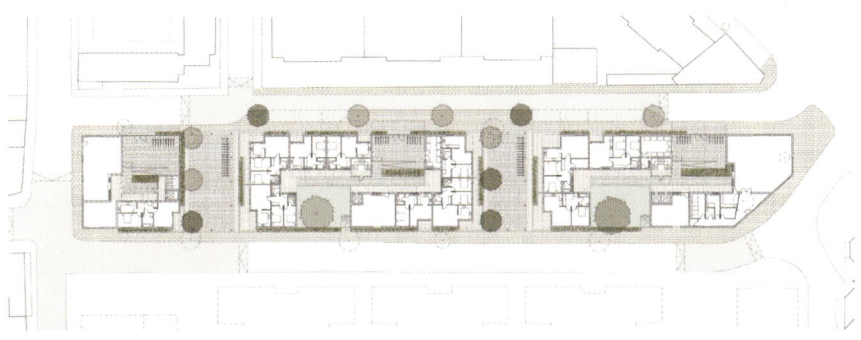
SITE PLAN

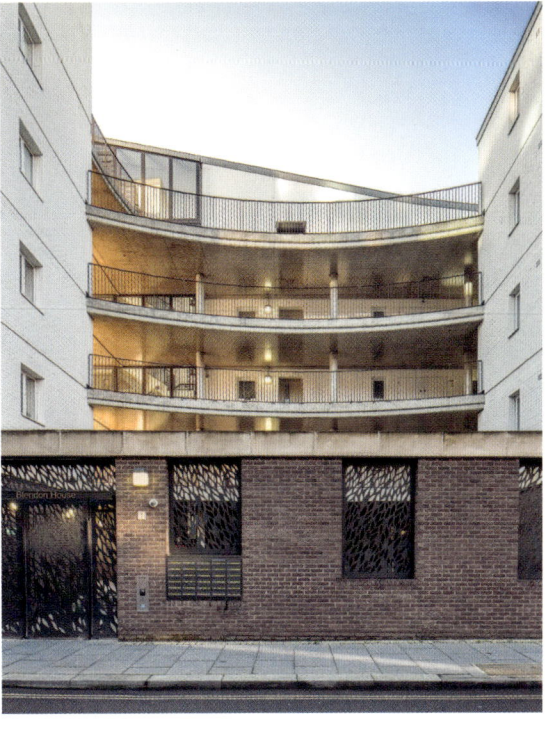

The site – which had been used as a car park for decades – now contains three residential blocks, a maximum of six storeys in height, which have a distinctive presence on the street.

Housing

Two Fifty One

ARCHITECT Allies and Morrison
DATE 2017
ADDRESS 251 Southwark Bridge Road, SE1 6FJ
CLIENT ECA Developments Ltd

Plans to redevelop the site of Eileen House, close to Elephant and Castle, were rejected by Southwark Council in 2011 after a petition objecting to the project received 50,000 signatures. Objections were fuelled by concerns that a residential development of the site would mean the closure of the Ministry of Sound, a hugely popular music venue in a former bus garage on nearby Gaunt Street. The proposed development was to replace an undistinguished eight-storey 1960s office block that had been used by South Bank University. Following the council's decision, the scheme was called in by the Mayor of London. It received planning consent in 2013 and was completed in 2017. (Following an agreement between the developer of Two Fifty One and the Ministry of Sound, the venue remains on the site it has occupied for two decades.)

Two Fifty One is a forty-one-storey tower containing 335 flats and the usual residents' amenities, including a restaurant, health club and cinema. An adjacent seven-storey block contains office and retail space, retaining the provision of employment on the site. The slender tower, with two façades clad in stone and a third fully glazed, forms a dramatic gateway to Elephant and Castle and has become a local landmark. The two lowest floors contain a large residents' foyer and office space, while the remainder of the tower has ten or twelve flats per floor, the largest enjoying a generous 250 square metres of living space around a central core. The angled geometry allows the provision of six winter gardens for the use of about half of the residents, while a public park at street level is a public benefit of the project.

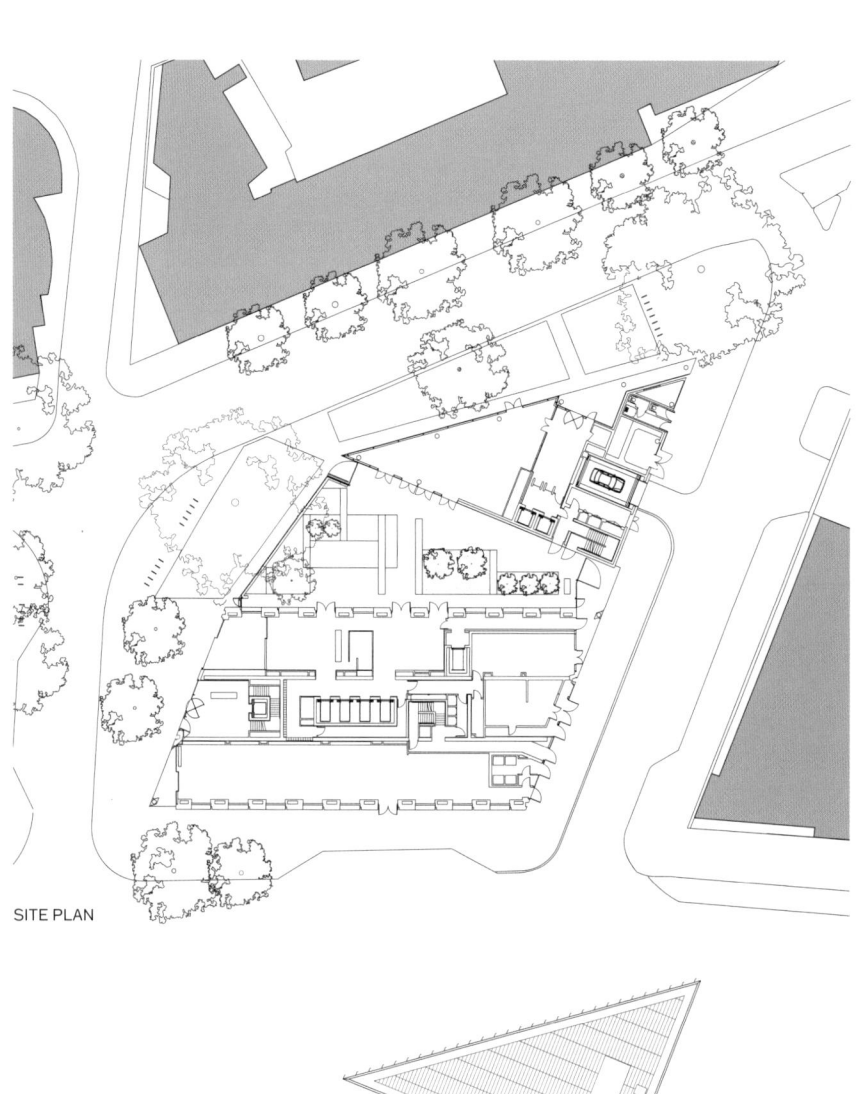
SITE PLAN

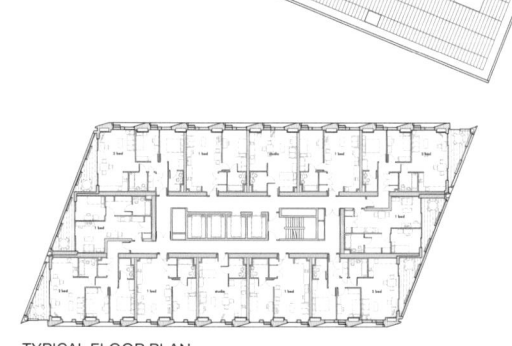
TYPICAL FLOOR PLAN

The forty-one-storey tower is a new presence on the skyline and streetscape of Elephant and Castle, and features a series of winter gardens among its amenities for residents.

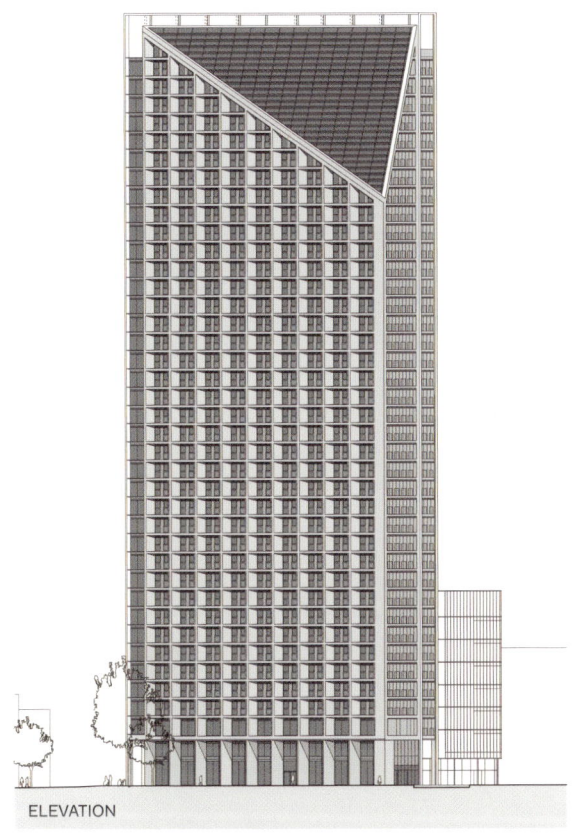

ELEVATION

81–87 Weston Street

ARCHITECT Allford Hall Monaghan Morris
DATE 2018
ADDRESS 81–87 Weston Street, SE1 3RS
CLIENTS Freshire Ltd | Solidspace

The client for this project in the hinterland south of London Bridge station was Roger Zogolovitch of Solidspace, architect turned developer, who argues that it combines 'contemporary materials and traditional manufacturing processes in order to regain the clarity of our familiar historic buildings in the setting of the city'.

The site for the development, containing eight flats plus 470 square metres of office space, adjoins a small park in an area where council housing is interspersed with warehouses and workshops – a classic inner-city mix. The building respects the established scale of Weston Street, stepping up from three to eight storeys, achieving maximum density while respecting context. The two- and three-bedroom, open-plan flats, arranged around two separate cores, are split section in form, on a series of intersecting half-levels. This strategy, which was pioneered by 1930s modernists, provides double-height living spaces with bedrooms stacked to form a dynamic whole. (Zogolovitch comments that 'the marriage of plan and section is the key to creating a sense of space'.) Extensive use of timber contrasts with exposed board-marked concrete to create interiors that are both dramatic and comfortable.

The exterior of the development is clad in brick on a concrete frame, with generous projecting balconies – large enough to accommodate a table and chairs – working in tandem with the stepped form that responds to planning constraints. Windows reflect the crafted approach of the project, manufactured in Italy and designed in tune with the strongly articulated form of the façades and with the mix of dynamic modernity and respect for tradition that drove its architectural strategy.

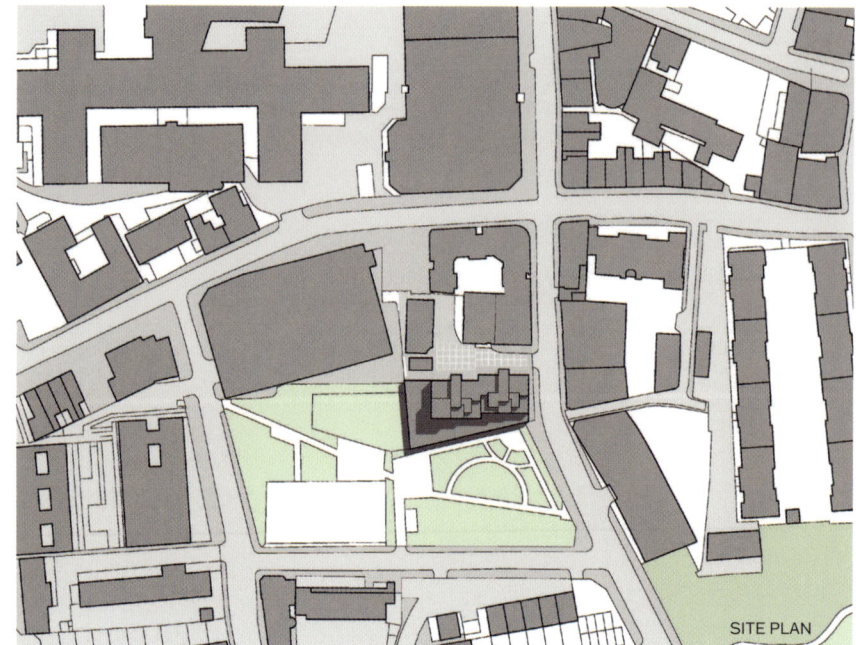

SITE PLAN

THREE-DIMENSIONAL VIEW

Modest in scale and a maximum of eight storeys in height, the development is innovative internally, with a split-section diagram that provides dramatic living spaces.

Housing

Infrastructure & Jobs

The dramatic renaissance that has taken place in Southwark in recent decades has been fuelled by major public transport projects, notably the Jubilee Line Extension, a driver of the emergence of the former Surrey Docks in Rotherhithe as a dynamic residential and leisure quarter. The reconstruction of London Bridge station, long London's least loved terminal, has transformed the surrounding area, with RPBW Architects' Shard as a landmark of renewal. Southwark is now a major base for offices, but small and new businesses are also finding a home in the borough. New businesses can find accommodation – at modest rents – at the Hithe in Rotherhithe, a development backed by funding from Southwark Council. At 53 and 55 Great Suffolk Street, long-neglected industrial buildings have been sensitively converted to office use, while the council worked with a developer to reinvent the former Walworth town hall and library as both a community hub and a home for small businesses.

'Fantastic. It's been really smartened up, made much more navigable.'

A TRAVELLER THROUGH LONDON BRIDGE STATION

53 and 55 Great Suffolk Street

ARCHITECT Hawkins\Brown
DATE 2017 (no. 53) | Under construction (no. 55)
ADDRESS 53/55 Great Suffolk Street, SE1 0DB
CLIENTS Morgan Capital Partners (no. 53) | Fabrix (no. 55)

These two rare survivals of the commercial world of nineteenth-century Bankside have, after long neglect, found new uses in tune with the area's dynamic renewal. Number 55 Great Suffolk Street, dating from about 1860, was listed Grade II in 2009. Built of brick, with timber floors supported on iron columns, it had been disused for decades, unaltered but dilapidated, before Hawkins\Brown's ongoing conversion project emerged.

To preserve the integrity of the historic structure, new services – WCs, a lift and a bike store – will be accommodated in a new core, connected to the existing building by bridge links and clad in corrugated metal. (Steel for the new structure is being recycled from a demolished building at Broadgate in the City.)

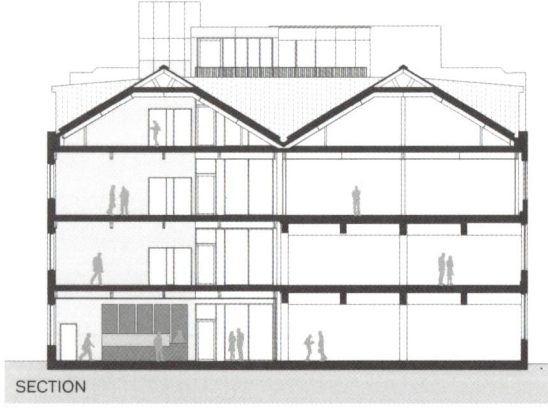

An open yard will provide a welcoming point of entrance from Loman Street. New steel staircases will link the floors internally, and the splendid timber roof structure is to be left dramatically exposed.

Across the side street, no. 53 is a modest building of the 1890s, unlisted and previously used for meat-processing and by a blacksmith. The project was made viable by the demolition of a single-storey addition and its replacement with a new extension that is appropriate in scale and materials, clad externally in salt-glazed brick. Internally, a staircase crafted of raw steel with brass fittings and set in a glazed enclosure connects all floors. The interiors retain the original industrial character, with painted brickwork, raw steel and concrete providing welcome relief from plasterboard. A generous roof terrace offers a breakout space with views across Southwark.

The two long-neglected warehouse buildings retain their industrial character after conversion. A new addition complementing the old in scale and materials is a feature of no. 53 (opposite). Its interior (below) is pleasant and spacious. At no. 55 (left), a new service core links to the old structure.

Infrastructure & Jobs

Employment Academy

ARCHITECT Peter Barber Architects
DATE 2013
ADDRESS 29 Peckham Road, SE5 8UA
CLIENT Thames Reach

AXONOMETRIC SKETCH

ELEVATION SKETCH

The Employment Academy, built for the Southwark-based charity Thames Reach, offers training and support services for the long-term unemployed. The academy is based in a listed Edwardian building designed by Edwin Thomas Hall – whose practice also designed Liberty's store – which was constructed as the offices of Southwark's Poor Law Guardians and later housed Southwark Council offices. Barber's practice was responsible for the conversion of the building, acquired by the charity in 2009, and for a substantial addition that is an eloquent expression of the practice's approach.

The listed building has an imposing elevation to Peckham Road. Inside are some impressive interiors, notably the former council chamber, accessed by a grand staircase. High-quality woodwork, mosaics and decorative tiling provide enrichment. The wing extending some 50 metres along Havil Street is more informal in appearance, with a picturesquely varied elevation that expresses the influence of the Arts and Crafts movement but with more workaday interiors reflecting its use as offices. As part of the project, the council chamber was converted into an events space with adjacent committee rooms – generous, light-filled spaces with ceilings 4 metres high – brought into use as meeting spaces and classrooms.

The office wing along Havil Street had suffered from a rear addition that shut out natural light and resulted in gloomy interiors. Its removal opened the way for the rehabilitation of the building, with offices for the charity and a community café, and the construction of a new L-shaped building around an open courtyard. A three-storey tower forms a marker on Havil Street for the new building, constructed of a light rustic brick, bonded with lime mortar, to contrast with the red brick used by Hall. Attached is a brick-vaulted structure – termed an exedra by the architects – which terminates the courtyard. It has no function, other than to provide an apt conclusion to the space. The entire project demonstrates Barber's inventive approach to the reinvention of traditional ways of building.

Barber's usual sensitivity and inventiveness are reflected in a project that repurposes a fine Edwardian listed building and adds a new wing in a manner that subtly recalls the Arts and Crafts manner.

Infrastructure & Jobs

Guy's Cancer Centre

ARCHITECT RSHP
DATE 2016
ADDRESS Great Maze Pond, SE1 3SS
CLIENT Guy's and St Thomas' NHS Foundation Trust

Guy's Hospital, one of London's leading teaching hospitals, occupies a complex of buildings dating from the time of its foundation in the 1720s onwards. Rooted on its historic location, the hospital has had to make the best possible use of its confined site in updating its building stock. Its Tower Wing, completed in 1974 and recently refurbished, remains one of the world's tallest hospital buildings. RSHP's 60-metre, fourteen-storey Cancer Centre makes optimum use of a tight site, forming a triangular landmark gateway to the hospital on Great Maze Pond.

The building reflects Guy's role as a centre for medical education as well as a place where patients are treated. It is conceived as a series of two- or three-storey 'care villages', each dealing with a particular aspect of patient treatment – radiotherapy, chemotherapy and a one-stop clinic housing diagnostic and outpatients' facilities – and each housing treatment rooms as well as seating and relaxation areas for patients. (The design of the latter draws on RSHP's experience with that of the Maggie's Centre at Charing Cross Hospital.) The chemotherapy village incorporates a floor occupied by researchers from King's College London. A double-height welcome area forms the base of the building. Clear wayfinding within the building is a key aspect of the scheme – in contrast to the tortuous routes that patients experience in many older hospitals.

The awkward site for the centre, with little storage space for materials and equipment, necessitated an innovative construction strategy. Largely prefabricated parts were used, with a unified cladding system applied to a concrete frame and services delivered as a modular package and connected once on the site. Set in a newly landscaped area, the building – which makes use of colourful external cladding, in the best RSHP tradition, to denote the internal zones – is an example of progressive architecture linked to innovative approaches to healthcare.

SECTION

SITE PLAN

Skilfully slotted into a small site on the Guy's campus, the new centre provides outstanding diagnostic and care facilities for cancer patients and space for researchers. Its architectural language, typical of RSHP, includes the generous use of colour.

Infrastructure & Jobs

Harold Moody Health Centre

ARCHITECT Morris + Company
DATE 2024
ADDRESS 60 Thurlow Street, SE17 2GB
CLIENTS London Borough of Southwark | Notting Hill Genesis

MODEL

EARLY YEARS NURSERY

The Harold Moody Health Centre is an element of the ongoing redevelopment of the Aylesbury estate, one of the largest housing schemes in Europe when it was completed in the 1970s. The health centre and a new public library (designed by HTA Design – the lead designer for the masterplan) are at the heart of the regeneration project, in line with a masterplan that concentrates community infrastructure on a site designated Plot 18, around a public space. Plot 18 is conceived as a civic centre, a local landmark serving both new and existing communities.

The health centre, which also houses an Early Years nursery, was designed after extensive consultation with stakeholders. The results fed into the design process, informing every element of the project, from the plan of the building to the position of furniture and internal colour schemes.

The strongly sculptural exterior of the freestanding building, punctuated by window openings, is formed of panels of prefabricated cast stone, pink in colour, warm and welcoming, and providing a deliberate contrast to the palette of surrounding buildings. Internally, the aim was to create barrier-free, welcoming access for patients, from the reception area

onwards. Generous floor-to-ceiling heights, wide corridors and an atrium connecting the two clinical levels are key to the ambition to create a calm healing environment, framed by views out and reinforced by the durable palette of warm materials that is used throughout the building. The needs of staff as well as of users were carefully considered, with office spaces allowing both focused and collaborative working, and meeting rooms and breakout spaces to provide for interaction between those who work in the building. The aim is to support the delivery of a more integrated healthcare service.

The Early Years facility on the upper level of the building, equipped with its own kitchen, was designed to deliver large, flexible open-plan learning spaces linked to an external play space with fine views across the city.

A key community gain from the ongoing redevelopment of the Aylesbury estate, the health centre features a generously scaled, barrier-free interior set around an atrium. The building exerts its public function through a powerfully modelled exterior in cast stone.

Infrastructure & Jobs

The Hithe

ARCHITECT IF_DO
DATE 2021
ADDRESS 71–75 Albion Street, SE16 7JA
CLIENT London Borough of Southwark

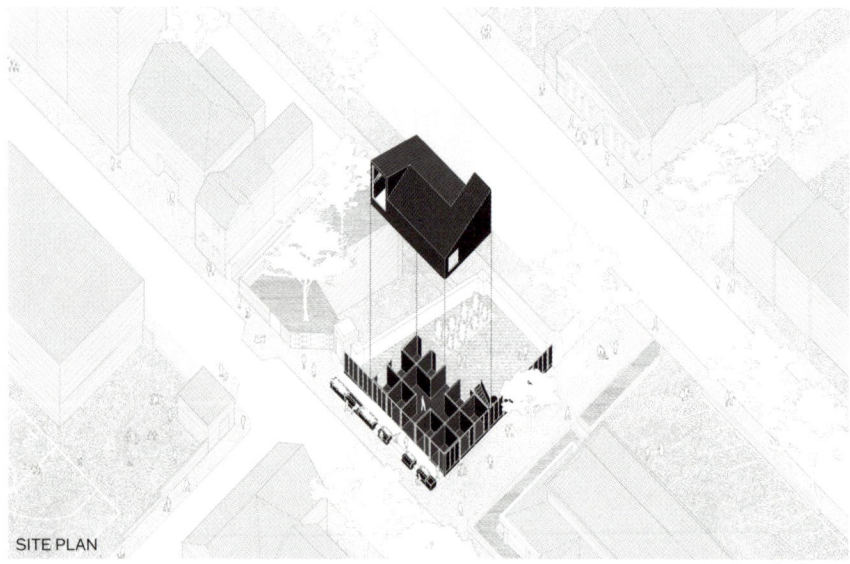
SITE PLAN

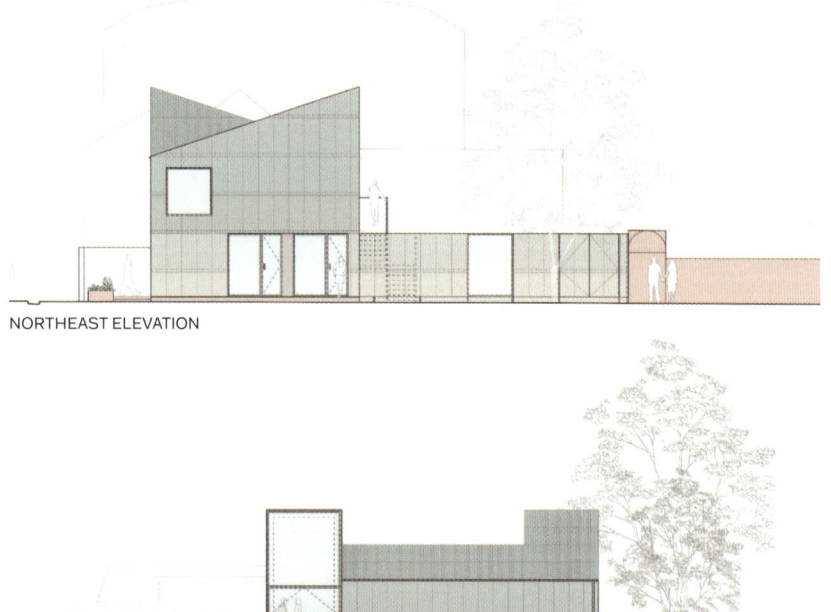
NORTHEAST ELEVATION

SOUTHEAST ELEVATION

The Hithe is an innovative, low-cost (£400,000) incubator space on Albion Street, Rotherhithe, for small businesses, commissioned by Southwark Council and developed in association with the pioneering social enterprise Meanwhile Space, which occupies one of the twelve workspace units in the building. It was the second project to be commissioned from IF_DO by Meanwhile Space, the first being a short-term refurbishment scheme at Lower Marsh, Waterloo, now closed.

This is a new departure for Meanwhile Space as a new-build space designed for future relocation and reuse. In its present location on Albion Street, it acts as a community hub in a part of the borough that is presently undergoing radical change.

The structure of The Hithe was designed in collaboration with engineer Elliott Wood and fabricator Weber Industries to be fully demountable and relocatable. It is constructed on a lightweight steel-and-timber frame, using some recycled materials, and sits on existing foundations, eliminating the need for new concrete on the site. Timber structure and services are left exposed, and the cladding is made of structural insulated panels. Ten studio spaces are arranged around a central social area, with links to the shared kitchen and to a planted outdoor gathering space. On the first floor are two larger units. All the workspaces (which total 200 square metres) are accessed directly from outside, removing the need for internal circulation. Double-height glazed lanterns on the north and south elevations make the building a landmark on the street.

At the time of writing, tenants of the scheme included an architect, a filmmaker and a beauty entrepreneur. Rents as low as £270 per month are designed to attract new enterprises, with an emphasis on those based in the locality.

The project offers affordable workspaces for small businesses. The building, constructed on a lightweight steel and timber frame, is designed to be demountable for possible relocation.

Infrastructure & Jobs

London Bridge Station

ARCHITECT Grimshaw
DATE 2018
ADDRESS London Bridge Street, SE1 9SG
CLIENT Network Rail

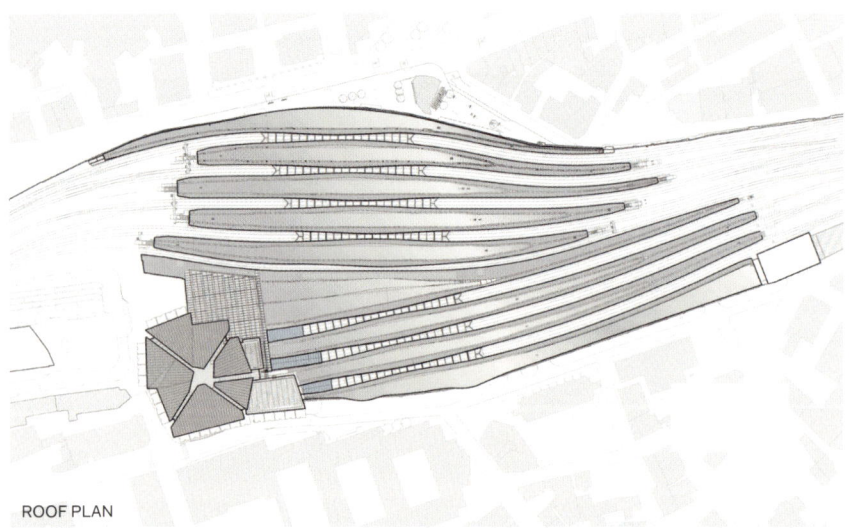
ROOF PLAN

That great railway enthusiast John Betjeman wrote of London Bridge station that 'one could hardly believe the misery its lack of accommodation, its narrow platforms and steep heart-testing steps have caused millions of Londoners for the last hundred years.' It was 'the most complicated, muddled and unwelcoming of all London termini', he said, the product of war damage followed in the 1960s by partial rebuilding. The opening of Thameslink services through London Bridge, Britain's fourth busiest railway station, made major reconstruction inevitable.

Grimshaw's project (structural engineers: WSP/Arcadis) necessitated the sacrifice of several historic elements, among them the impressive 1860s Brighton train shed and the former railway offices on Tooley Street. The £1 billion redevelopment, informed by a masterplan drawn up by TP Bennett and Alan Baxter Partnership in 2000, went on site in 2012 and was carried out with train services continuing to operate throughout.

A fundamental aspect of the project was to provide a new ground-level concourse, an impressive civic space 80 metres wide and 165 metres long, naturally ventilated and naturally lit, with shops and cafés for commuters. Far removed from the depressing airport-style Euston station, the concourse is a meeting place – not just for travellers – and forms a connection between two quarters of

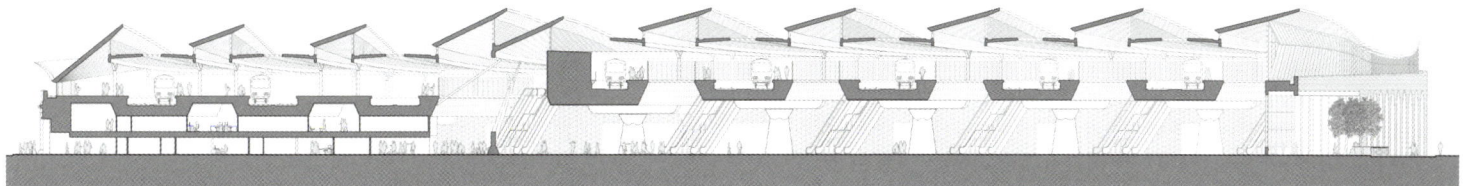

LONGITUDINAL SECTION

Southwark formerly divided by the railway, with major points of entry on St Thomas Street and Tooley Street. The Western Arcade forms another link, taking the line of the former Joiner Street and tripling its length with the brick arches of the station's undercroft exposed. The arcade connects the concourse to the heavily used Underground station.

The platforms above, accessed by escalators, are covered by dramatically formed roofs, compared by the architects to a 'giant urban sculpture', a counterpoint to the Shard (page 104) towering above. Daylight flows through from the platforms into the concourse, and timber-lined soffits provide visual warmth and soften the functional aesthetic of the space.

The new London Bridge is a railway station with a profound impact on the city. It not only offers vastly improved facilities for travellers, but also creates a new focus for the surrounding area, linking previously divided communities.

The reconstruction has transformed the station into a new focus for the surrounding area as well as radically improving the travelling experience.

Infrastructure & Jobs

King's College Hospital Campus

Fetal Medicine Research Institute
ARCHITECT A21 Architects
DATE 2017
ADDRESS 16–20 Windsor Walk, SE5 8BB
CLIENT The Fetal Medicine Foundation

King's College Hospital moved from central London to Denmark Hill just before the First World War, and over more than a century many buildings have been added to its campus. The Fetal Medicine Research Institute, occupied by the hospital and the Fetal Medicine Foundation (which funded the project), is the most recent addition. The 5,225-square-metre building housing the institute, adjacent to Denmark Hill station, provided a new state-of-the-art base for the world-renowned Harris Birthright Centre, caring for more than 10,000 patients a year.

The building contains consulting and treatment rooms, ultrasound scanning facilities, research laboratories, lecture and meeting rooms, and associated administrative offices – a complex mix in a building providing both patient care and advanced research and teaching. It is a landmark in a largely Victorian context. Columns extending from the ground curve to form an arched roof, enclosing the main public and clinical spaces, while a glazed atrium provides a welcoming, light-filled point of entry.

Ortus

ARCHITECT Morris + Company
DATE 2013
ADDRESS 82–96 Grove Lane, SE5 8SN
CLIENT Maudsley Charity

Ortus, a learning centre commissioned by the Maudsley Charity – which is dedicated to promoting public awareness of mental health – is close to Denmark Hill station, within the campus of King's College Hospital. Morris + Company's building has been described as 'an elegant oasis of openness', reflecting the charity's objectives. It provides 1,500 square metres of space over seven levels and is open to all five days a week; offering facilities for meetings, conferences, lectures and training courses, it is a facility for both the public and the medical profession. (The ground-floor café, which spills out on to a paved public space, is popular among locals, as well as students and staff from the hospital.)

The architecture of the building, externally staggered from three to four storeys across a sloping site, is a model of calm and elegance, with a simplicity and directness that mirror Maudsley's philosophy of openness and welcome. Externally it is a freestanding pavilion, almost Georgian in its calm restraint, with a grid of precast concrete framing panels of full-height glazing and warm brick (variegated in hue and left exposed in much of the interior). The ethos of openness is fundamental to the internal character of the building, which is timber-floored and steeped in natural light, with a stairwell rising from the stepped ground-floor auditorium that adapts for a wide range of events. This is a building that responds strongly to the aims of the client in its openness and sense of welcome.

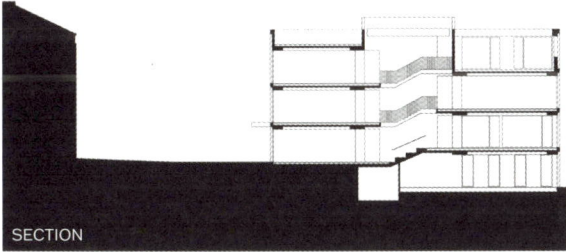
SECTION

The Fetal Medicine Research Institute (opposite) combines patient care and advanced research in a building focused on a glazed atrium under a striking arched roof. Ortus (this page) is a facility for both the public and the medical profession, with architecture that is appropriately calm and welcoming.

Infrastructure & Jobs

160 Tooley Street

ARCHITECT Allford Hall Monaghan Morris
DATE 2009
ADDRESS 160 Tooley Street, SE1 2QH
CLIENT Great Portland Estates

The headquarters of Southwark Council since 2009, number 160 Tooley Street offers a progressive vision of the way office buildings can respond to the urgent need for a sustainable architecture. The site, squeezed between Tooley Street and the railway tracks into London Bridge station, was occupied by three Victorian commercial buildings, not listed but of some interest as reflecting the history of the area. Low-rise industrial sheds were squeezed in at the rear, adjacent to the railway.

The developer Great Portland Estates obtained planning consent in 2006 for a project that combined refurbishment and new-build to create a building of 18,600 square metres containing five floors of flexible office space, five residential units, and a number of shops on the ground floor. Sustainability was a key objective in the development of the project, with solar heating, intelligent lighting systems, recycled water, low-maintenance finishes, a displacement air-conditioning system and the cooling effects of an exposed concrete structure working to reduce energy costs. The optimum use of natural light was a prime objective, reflected in the design of the new elevations. The use of prefabricated structural components, with minimal use of 'wet' trades (those that involve materials mixed with water, such as concrete and plaster) and extensive use of self-finished materials, kept costs down. The prefabrication of services simplified the construction process further.

The existing buildings on Tooley Street were retained, refurbished and cut away to incorporate them in the development. The entrance leads into a full-height, daylit four-storey atrium topped by an ETFE roof, a striking new addition to a project that combines conversion and new-build to create a reinterpretation of the 'warehouse aesthetic' tailored to twenty-first-century needs.

SOUTH ELEVATION

NORTH ELEVATION

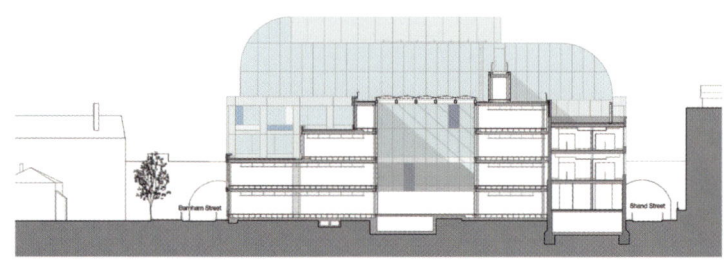
CROSS SECTION THROUGH ATRIUM

The building incorporates the retained façades of three Victorian commercial buildings (opposite, bottom). Behind is a daylit atrium (left), the heart of a project that combines reuse and new-build to striking effect in a structure that exemplifies the Southwark of the twenty-first century.

Infrastructure & Jobs

Walworth Town Hall and Central Library

PROPOSED ELEVATION

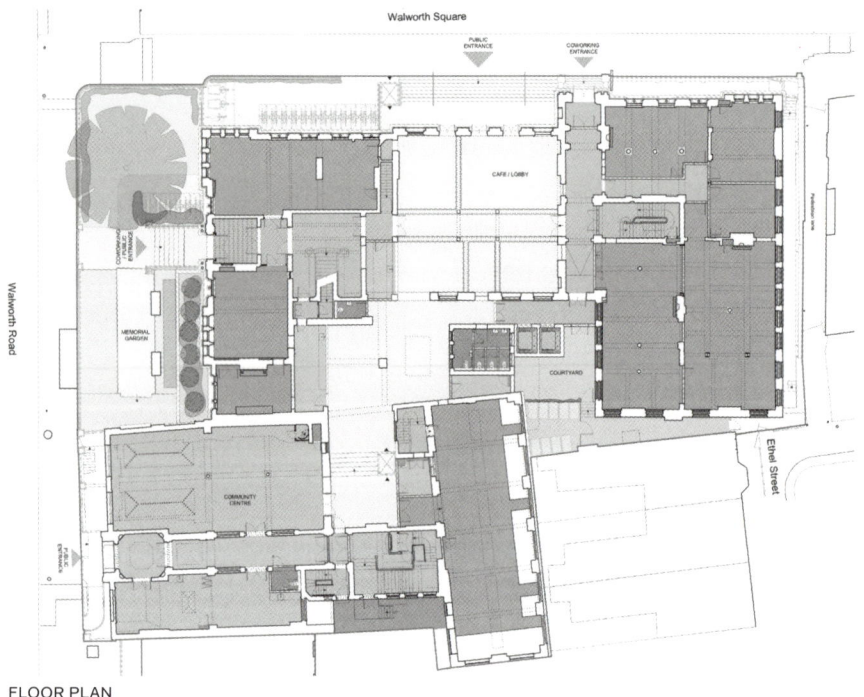
FLOOR PLAN

The long-neglected town hall and library on Walworth Road have been repurposed and sensitively refurbished, with original features carefully restored.

Taste in architecture – as in everything else – changes. In 1983 *The Buildings of England* dismissed Walworth town hall (by Henry Jarvis, 1866; extended in 1902) and the adjacent library (Edward I'Anson, 1893) as, respectively, 'sadly Gothic' and 'insignificant'. They are now listed buildings, but were disposed of by Southwark Council (the library moving to a new building on Walworth Road, designed by architect AOC as part of the Elephant Park project; see page 134). A fire in 2013 caused significant damage to the upper storey of the town hall, and the former council chamber was gutted.

Feix & Merlin's project, developed with Donald Insall Associates as historic buildings consultant, sought to regenerate the buildings in tune with the regeneration of the Elephant and Castle Opportunity Area. Working in collaboration with Southwark Council, the developer, General Projects, aimed to create a new employment hub for small and medium-sized businesses, along with a community centre and café, with major interior spaces, such as the former council chamber and reference library, available for public use. The aim was to revitalize the building as a resource for the area, while making minimal alterations to its fabric.

The principal point of entrance to the former town hall was relocated away from the busy Walworth Road to the new square alongside the building. A generous new stair provides access, linked to a lift for use by disabled people. Inside, the ground floor, with a café open to all, is connected to the library, where a new community centre on the ground floor is seen as the heart of the revitalized complex. Three 'flexi-rooms' are available for a variety of community uses, ranging from art classes to yoga sessions. A new lift core serves both buildings, now brought together as a unified complex. A new floor in a previously unused loft space above the eastern part of the town hall provides further office space, and there is a new mezzanine on the first floor. The services and plant of both buildings were totally renewed.

The relatively intact – though dilapidated – spaces within the library were the subject of

ARCHITECT Feix & Merlin
DATE 2024
ADDRESS 147 Walworth Road, SE17 1RS
CLIENT General Projects

a light-touch refurbishment, and some internal divisions were removed. Protective boxing was stripped off to reveal original internal finishes and features, and, in line with Historic England's advice, the impressive main staircase was carefully restored. The third floor of the building was opened up as office space.

The project is a carefully considered balance of renewal and restoration. The temporary roof of the town-hall extension of 1902, for instance, installed after the destruction of the original roof in the fire, was replaced with Westmorland slates. A restored internal courtyard and new first-floor terrace provide breakout space for the users of a complex that has been inspiringly renewed as a focus for local business and community life.

Infrastructure & Jobs

Mixed Use

Cities are places where a mix of uses – housing, shops, offices and public buildings – exist and prosper in close proximity. The post-war reconstruction of London created too many areas where that mixture was lost. In Southwark, Elephant and Castle is an example, and the ongoing reconstruction of the area aims to reinstate a balanced mixture of uses, with private and public sectors working together. At Blackfriars Circus, a major residential development of both private and affordable homes also provides offices in a block shared with flats. The development of Bankside Yards, close to Blackfriars Bridge, meanwhile, mixes offices, private and social housing, and retail in a dynamic way, bringing a new vitality to the riverside. The Shard, London's most spectacular tall building, is the focus of a new quarter where offices and residential space combine with a major hotel and retail space to create a healthy blend of uses.

'It's a great community space with lots going on, flexible and well designed.'

A VISITOR TO THE NUNHEAD GREEN COMMUNITY CENTRE

Bankside Yards

ARCHITECTS Allies and Morrison | MAKE Architects | PLP Architecture | Stiff + Trevillion
DATE 2011–35
ADDRESS Southwark Street/Blackfriars Road, SE1
CLIENT Native Land

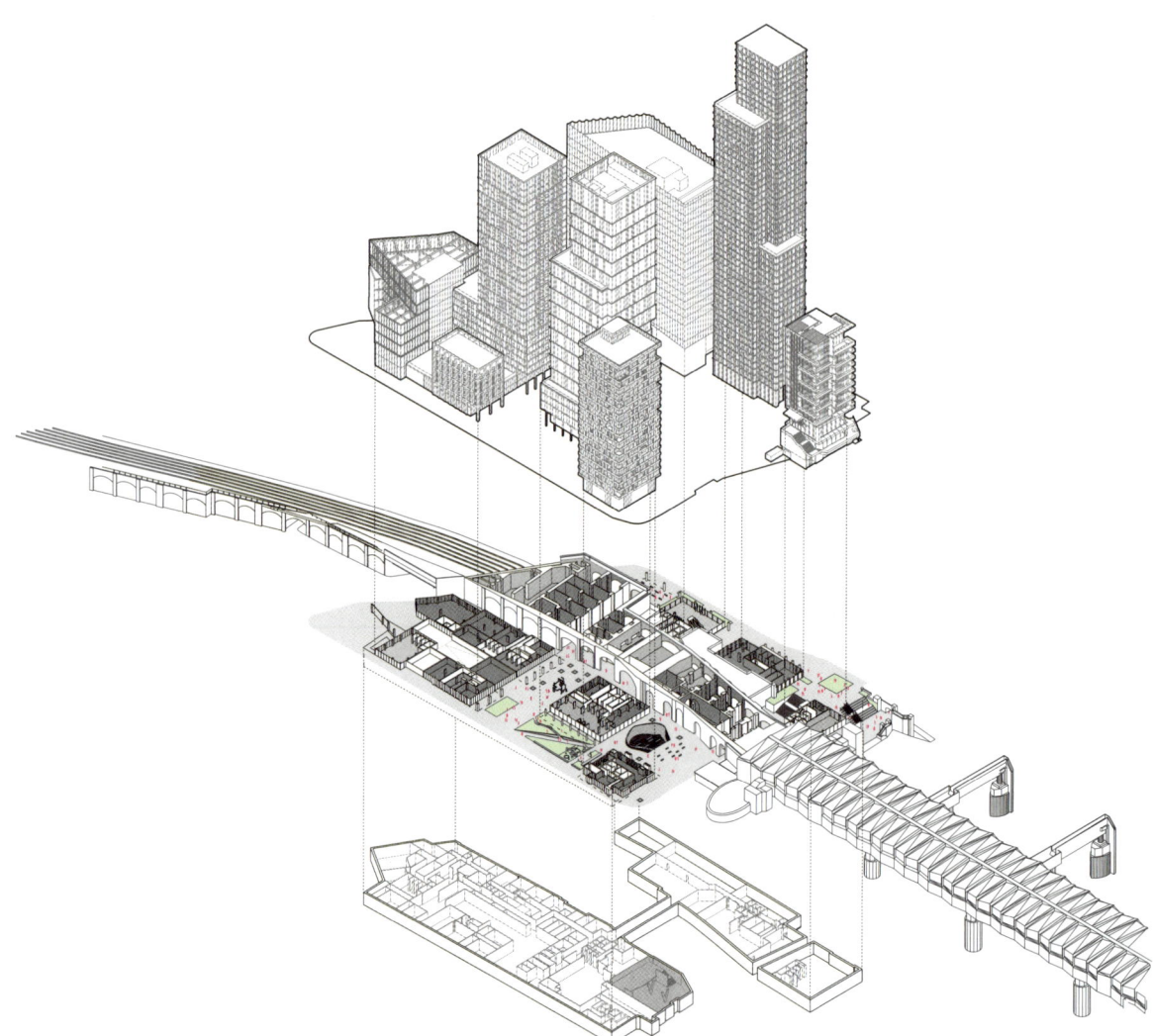

Promoted as 'London's new cultural neighbourhood', the Bankside Yards development occupies a key site by Blackfriars Bridge and forms a link in a chain of arts and cultural venues extending along the Thames from the Southbank Centre to Tate Modern and Shakespeare's Globe.

The site was previously occupied by two undistinguished and divisive blocks either side of the railway that runs on an elevated line through Blackfriars station. The development aims to create 'Britain's first fossil fuel-free mixed-use estate'. An important element in the development is Arbor, a nineteen-storey, 22,700-square-metre office building, completed in 2023, squeezed between Blackfriars Road and the railway and providing flexible workspaces aimed at a wide range of businesses. Similar provision for small enterprises is provided within the masterplan for the eastern yards.

Six buildings in the development house a total of more than 600 flats set in a network of public spaces focused on a central square. One of the eastern blocks will house the Mandarin Oriental hotel, which is scheduled to open in 2028. The residential towers vary in height, mediating between the landmark One Blackfriars tower (page 58) and the more modest scale of neighbouring developments. The tallest tower is of 50 storeys, containing 249 flats.

The arches carrying the railway are opened up to contain shops and restaurants and to provide new connections to neighbouring streets and transport facilities. A major gateway to the site and the surrounding area is provided by the southern entrance to Blackfriars station, which opened in 2011.

The sizeable development, straddling a busy railway line, will contain a mix of offices, flats, shops, restaurants and a hotel, and open a previously inaccessible stretch of the riverside connecting the Southbank Centre, Tate Modern and Shakespeare's Globe. Provision for small businesses is a feature of the project.

Mixed Use

Blackfriars Circus

ARCHITECT Maccreanor Lavington
DATE 2019
ADDRESS St George's Circus, SE1 8EH
CLIENT Kuropatwa Ltd

The Blackfriars Circus development occupies a site on Blackfriars Road fronting St George's Circus, the point where five major routes – those leading to Lambeth, Westminster, Waterloo, Blackfriars and Southwark bridges – meet. The spot is marked by an obelisk of 1771 designed by the Scottish architect Robert Mylne (also responsible for the present Blackfriars Bridge).

The project was designed with regard to the context of the St George's Circus Conservation Area, designated in 2000 following the listing of a number of buildings there. A key principle of the scheme was the need to respond to the existing scale and form of the Circus, embracing its curvilinear form and reasserting its significance.

The development incorporates various uses. Four mixed-use buildings are grouped around a courtyard with links to surrounding streets. A continuous retail frontage addresses Blackfriars Road, with broad new pavements. A twenty-eight-storey residential tower, hexagonal in form, is the landmark feature of the project, cut back at its upper levels to accentuate its verticality. It is topped by a crown of precast

concrete pinnacles. On the twenty-fifth and twenty-sixth floors, penthouses – open-plan and benefiting from higher ceilings – are provided, with winter gardens offering exceptional views.

At the northern end of the development, on Blackfriars Road, a brick-clad eight-storey building provides fifty-six affordable homes. Its two-storey base is clad in green and white brick, a nod to London tradition. The adjacent nine-storey block provides private and shared-ownership flats. Again, brick is used to good effect, with white glazed brick on the setback top storey, where residents have access to private terraces. The four-storey block opening on to the public courtyard is clad in grey brick. It provides two storeys of offices with flats above. The southernmost building in the development features a curved façade that reinstates the lost frontage of St George's Circus.

The development represents a considered attempt to respond to and repair the historic townscape and create a new neighbourhood that is a convincing exercise in urban design and, within the parameters of commercial development, creates a socially mixed community.

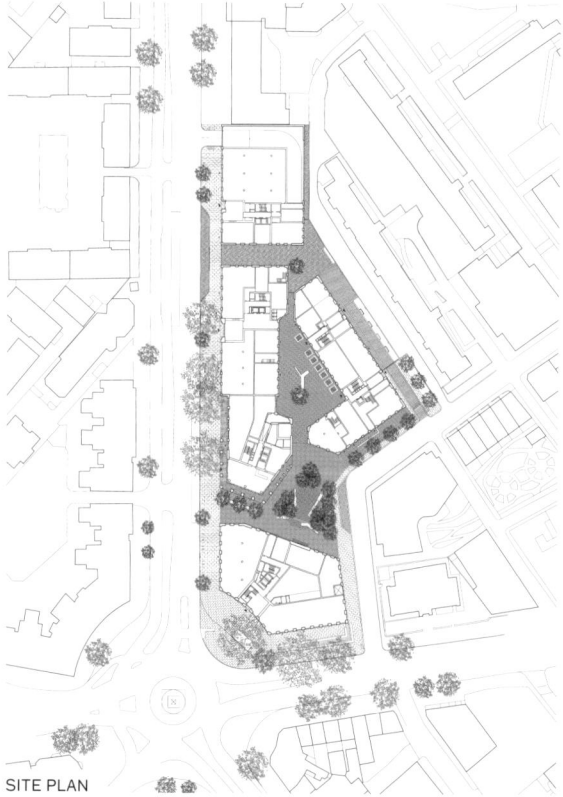

SITE PLAN

The dominant element is the hexagonal-form residential tower, but the project includes offices and mixed-tenure housing as well. It also restores the damaged form of St George's Circus (top right), a key development of the late eighteenth century.

Mixed Use

Elephant and Castle Town Centre

ARCHITECT Allies and Morrison
DATE 2020s
ADDRESS New Kent Road/Walworth Road/Newington Butts/St George's Road/London Road/Newington Causeway, SE17
CLIENTS Get Living | Delancey

Before the Second World War, when much of the area was levelled by German bombs, Elephant and Castle was described as 'the Piccadilly Circus of south London'. Theatres, cinemas, a department store and shops made it a focus of south London life. The post-war reconstruction included a covered shopping centre, which opened in 1965, the imposition of major roads that destroyed any sense of place, and a network of unwelcoming subterranean walkways.

The Elephant is now the focus of a massive reconstruction project that includes the demolition and redevelopment of the nearby Heygate housing estate and the development of Elephant Park (page 134). It is well connected – by two Underground lines, a mainline station and many bus routes – but these transport links were not integrated; the two Tube lines were served by unconnected stations, and bus stops were scattered around the area. The reconstruction of the Underground station will better connect the Northern and Bakerloo lines, and provide an integrated bus station.

The demolition in 2021 of the 1960s shopping centre was a landmark in the renewal

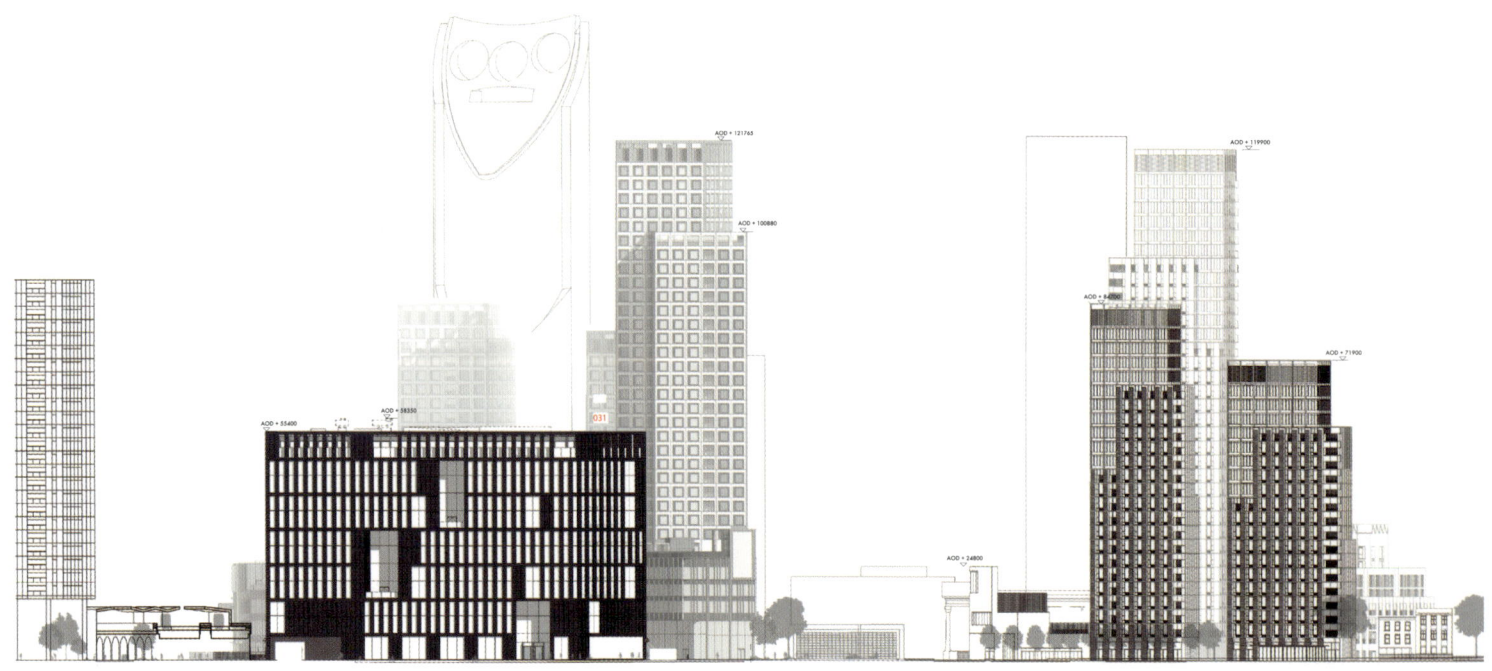

ELEVATION

94 Mixed Use

The redevelopment involved the demolition of the 1960s shopping centre. As part of the renewal of the area, London College of Communication will be rehoused in a dramatic new building on the site of the shopping centre (below and bottom).

project, and Developer Delancey created a new retail site at Castle Square for displaced tenants. The site of the old shopping centre will house the new 34,400-square-metre home of London College of Communication (LCC), now part of the University of the Arts London (UAL), as well as the administrative offices of UAL. The first three levels of the landmark building, built over an entrance to the Underground, will be publicly accessible, with retail and food outlets serving the college and the local community. It is designed for flexibility in line with LCC's developing curriculum. The LCC building will be the centrepiece of a family of buildings, including residential towers up to thirty-two storeys high, and shops. A new cinema and a home for the archive of the legendary filmmaker Stanley Kubrick are included in the LCC project.

The completion of this phase of the project will open the way for the demolition of LCC's existing 1960s complex and the redevelopment of that site, scheduled for completion in 2030, with nearly 500 new homes in blocks of up to 35 storeys, plus retail units.

Mixed Use

Nunhead Green

ARCHITECT AOC Architecture
DATE 2020
ADDRESS Nunhead Green, SE15 3QQ
CLIENTS London Borough of Southwark | One Housing

Nunhead Green was described in *The Buildings of England* (1983) as 'a pathetic scrap of grass and asphalt'. In 2007 it became the centre of a Conservation Area designated by Southwark Council, an urban quarter of modest Victorian terraces, an oasis amid large post-war housing developments. Appointed by Southwark Council in 2011 to develop a masterplan for the area, including the development of two vacant sites in council ownership, AOC engaged extensively with the community to explore how the area could be enhanced to meet local needs.

The long-neglected green space at the heart of the area formed the basis of AOC's first project. A once well-maintained amenity had degenerated into the 'pathetic scrap' described by Nikolaus Pevsner, used mainly by dog-walkers. The aim was to provide spaces that met local needs: an enclosed children's play area, a secluded garden, and a public square for community events. The Green, for all its modest scale, is now the true heart of the area.

The new community centre across the road was the next of AOC's projects to be completed. The architects concede a Post-modernist influence on its design, but its brick exterior is in tune with the character of the area, where the principal landmarks are a Tudorbethan pub and a listed group of Victorian almshouses. Housing a variety of activities, the building also provides space for local organizations and private parties, and has become a community hub. The interiors are timber-lined, daylit and subtly colourful, with a domestic rather than an institutional feel. The building is designed for economy, with an innovative 'dynamically insulated' wall system.

The third project, completed in 2020, is a housing development overlooking the Green. It consists of a terrace of eight family houses and a four-storey corner block containing six flats and maisonettes, some designed to meet the needs of disabled people. Constructed of red brick, the development features a variety of mortars, bonds and details in response to its neighbours, and steps down to match the height of the adjacent community hall. Topped by tall chimneys designed as service flues, it offers a new vision of housing in London.

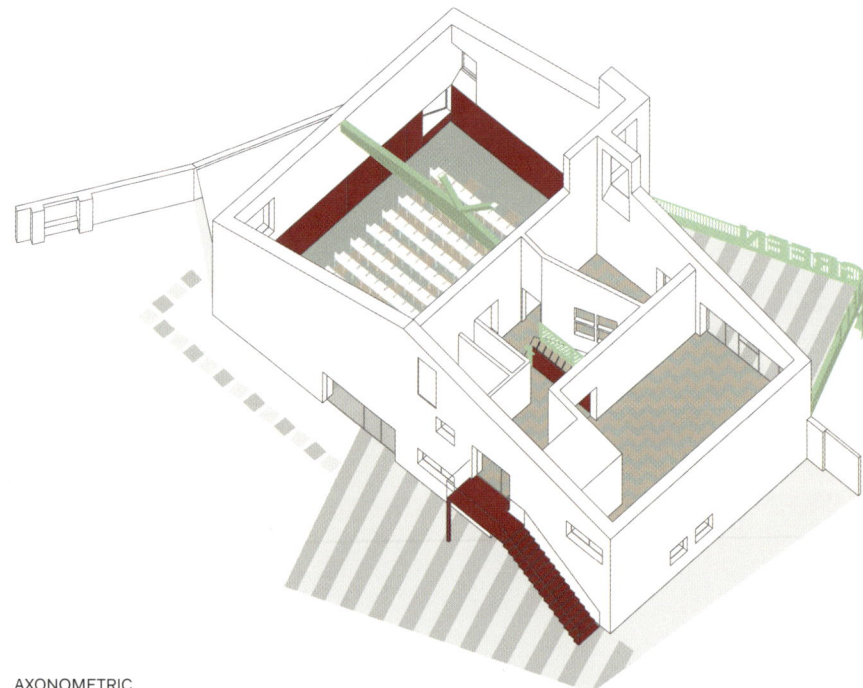

AXONOMETRIC

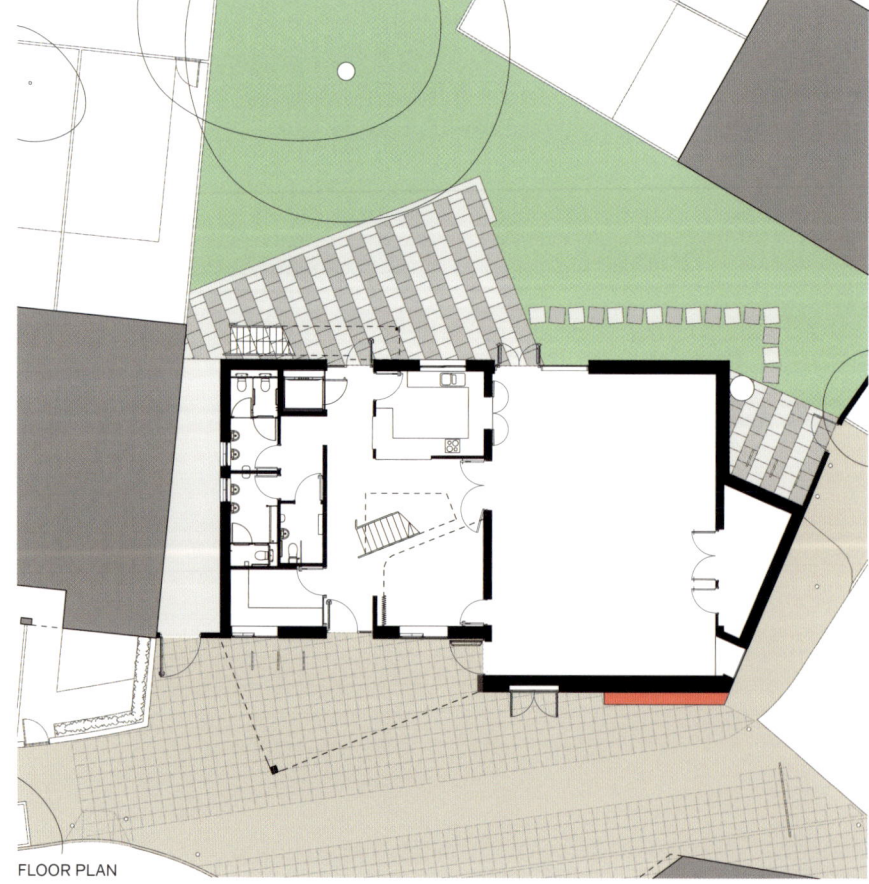

FLOOR PLAN

Nunhead Green, once little more than a piece of waste ground, was turned into a resource for local people as part of a comprehensive project that included the construction of a Post-modernist-influenced community centre.

Mixed Use

Southbank Tower

ARCHITECT KPF
DATE 2017
ADDRESS 55 Upper Ground, SE1 9EY
CLIENT King's Reach Estates

Completed in 1978, King's Reach Tower was a product of the last phase of the architect Richard Seifert's extraordinary career, which transformed the skyline of London. Built after the developer won a public inquiry – the area had been zoned as 'waterside and industrial' – the building, with its thirty storeys of offices sitting on a five-storey podium, suffered from a plan that provided a large central core and rather mean (900 square metres) office spaces. Vacated in 2004, the building was the subject of an unexecuted remodelling project before planning consent was given in 2011 for a mixed-use conversion. The addition of extra floors would bring the height of the tower to 155 metres, and a condition provided for the existing amount of employment space to be retained.

Underlining how far Seifert's original vision for the site had been cut back in execution, the project aimed to retain the best elements of the existing scheme while addressing its failings. Retaining the total area of office use on the site demanded the addition of eleven storeys to the tower and three storeys to the podium block. KPF's completed scheme provides 16,165 square metres of office space, 20,160 square metres of residential accommodation and 4,900 square metres of retail space. The massing of the extended tower was considered carefully. An analysis of its structure allowed a 9 per cent reduction in the area of the central core, allowing bathrooms for the flats to be located within that regained area. The office space in the base of the tower and the podium block was maximized by the removal of service cores at the end of the floorplates. The retail spaces take advantage of a new pedestrian route through the site between Upper Ground and Stamford Street, capitalizing on the proximity of the development to the riverside. Office users and residents have the use of three garden spaces between levels 1 and 10.

KPF's transformation of the tower and its subsidiary podium block has transformed a building that was unpopular with both its users and the public into a new landmark. This apparently hopelessly dated building has been reconfigured, providing a mixed-use development that is an elegant addition to Southwark's riverside.

The 1970s King's Reach Tower was one of the least successful of Richard Seifert's many high-rise projects, and remained empty for nearly a decade before being redeveloped. KPF's scheme raised the height of the tower by eleven storeys and has introduced a new mix of uses to the site.

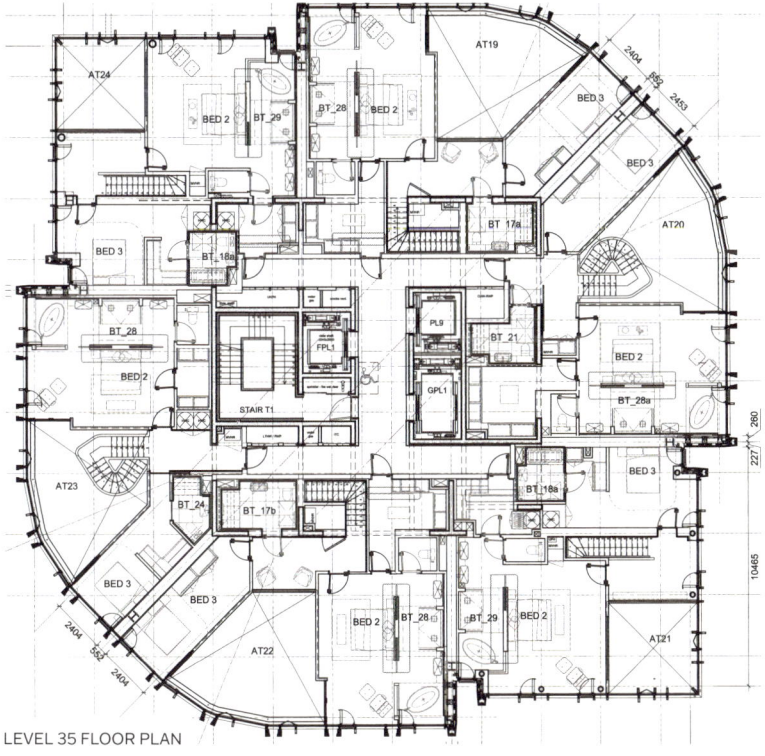

LEVEL 35 FLOOR PLAN

Mixed Use

Maple Quays and Ontario Point

ARCHITECT Howells
DATE 2013
ADDRESS Surrey Quays Road/Albatross Way, SE16 7EE
CLIENT Barratt London

The project is a key element in the renewal of the former Surrey Docks. Ontario Point residential tower (right) next to Canada Water station is a new landmark.

The Maple Quays development, which includes the twenty-six-storey Ontario Point tower with retail space at ground level, is next to Canada Water Tube station at the hub of renewal in the former area of Surrey Docks. Designed within the provisions of a masterplan by the Canadian consultant Urban Strategies Inc., it provides a total of 668 mixed-tenure residential units. The site was recognized as being of key importance in unlocking the potential of the surrounding area.

The development consists of three groups of 6–8-storey buildings set around landscaped courtyards, with the landmark tower at the apex of the site, close to the station and Deal Porter Square framing CZWG's public library (page 20). Marking a significant departure from the outline planning consent, it was

SITE PLAN

The remainder of the development consists of lower-rise housing (below), clad in brick, set around landscaped courtyards.

Mixed Use

101

the outcome of a twelve-month public consultation process that resulted in a denser project, and one more closely integrated into the surrounding neighbourhood.

The Ontario Point tower, 87 metres tall, is triangular in form, and all flats are provided with winter gardens in the angles. The three courtyard blocks are clad in brick, with timber elements, referencing the history of the area and drawing on the design tradition of dockland warehouses. The result is a family of buildings with a convincing sense of local identity.

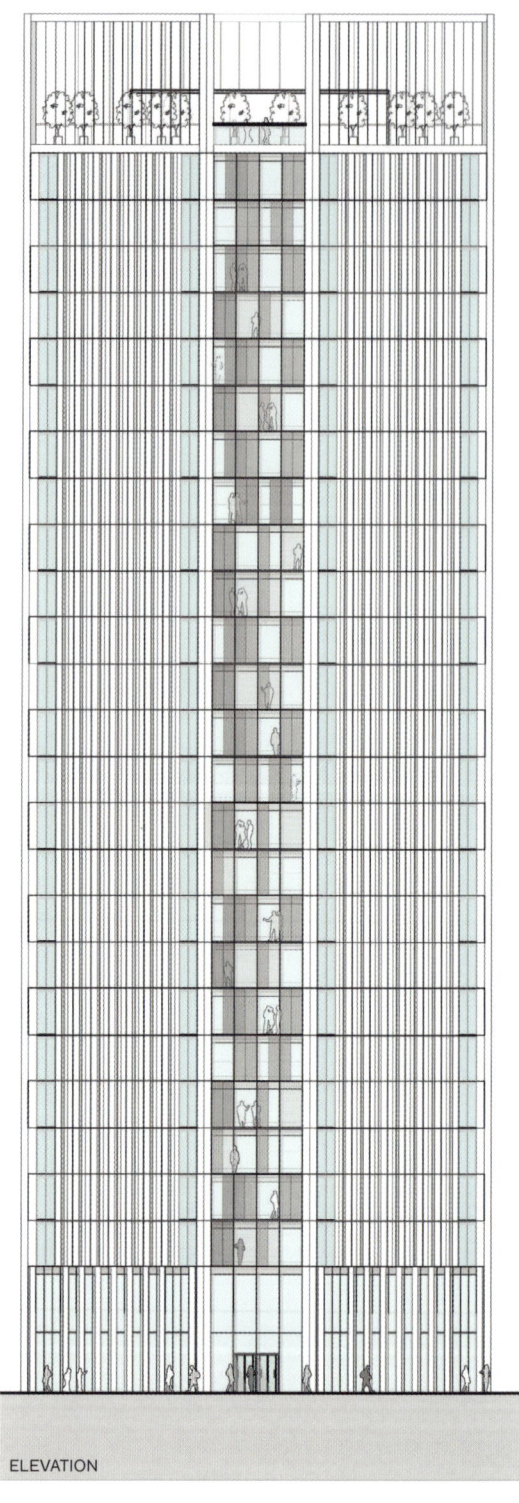

ELEVATION

The tower is one of London's most striking residential high rises, immaculately detailed and memorable in form.

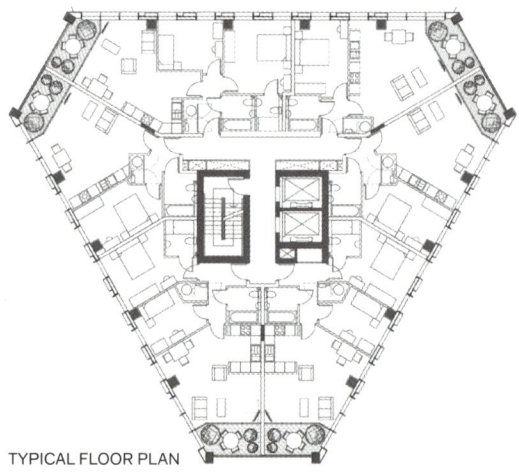

TYPICAL FLOOR PLAN

Mixed Use

The Shard Quarter

The Shard

ARCHITECT RPBW Architects
DATE 2013
ADDRESS 32 London Bridge Street, SE1 9SG
CLIENT Sellar Property Group

The Shard, designed by leading global architect Renzo Piano, is arguably the most popular – and certainly the most prominent – of all the high-rise buildings completed in London in the last quarter of a century. It is the centrepiece of a group of towers designed by Piano, forming the Shard Quarter, close to London Bridge station (page 80) and replacing two earlier high-rise buildings: Richard Seifert's London Bridge House of 1962; and TP Bennett's Southwark Towers of 1975. The developer was Irvine Sellar (1934–2017), with major investment from Qatari sources.

The project, which was opposed by Historic England and the Commission for Architecture and the Built Environment, won approval following a planning inquiry in 2003. (Historic England described the proposed tower as 'a shard of glass through the heart of historic London' – hence the subsequent name.)

Construction began on the Shard – 72 storeys, 310 metres high, the tallest building in western Europe – in 2009. Clad in extra-white glazing, the building has eight sloping façades that fragment its scale and generate its powerfully sculptural form. The façades are formed of double skins of glass (11,000 panes in total), naturally ventilated, with internal blinds that respond automatically to changing light levels.

The form of the building might appear arbitrary, but it expresses its various uses. Offices let to about thirty companies, and a private health clinic, occupy 55,740 square metres of space over the lower twenty-eight floors, and each office floor has access to winter gardens with opening windows. Levels 31–4 are occupied by restaurants. The Shangri-La hotel on levels 35–52, with 202 guest rooms, includes a spectacular infinity pool with panoramic

Controversial when first proposed, the Shard is now one of London's most popular landmarks. It contains flats, offices and a hotel – a virtual high-rise village – and the viewing gallery offers spectacular views, extending as far as Heathrow.

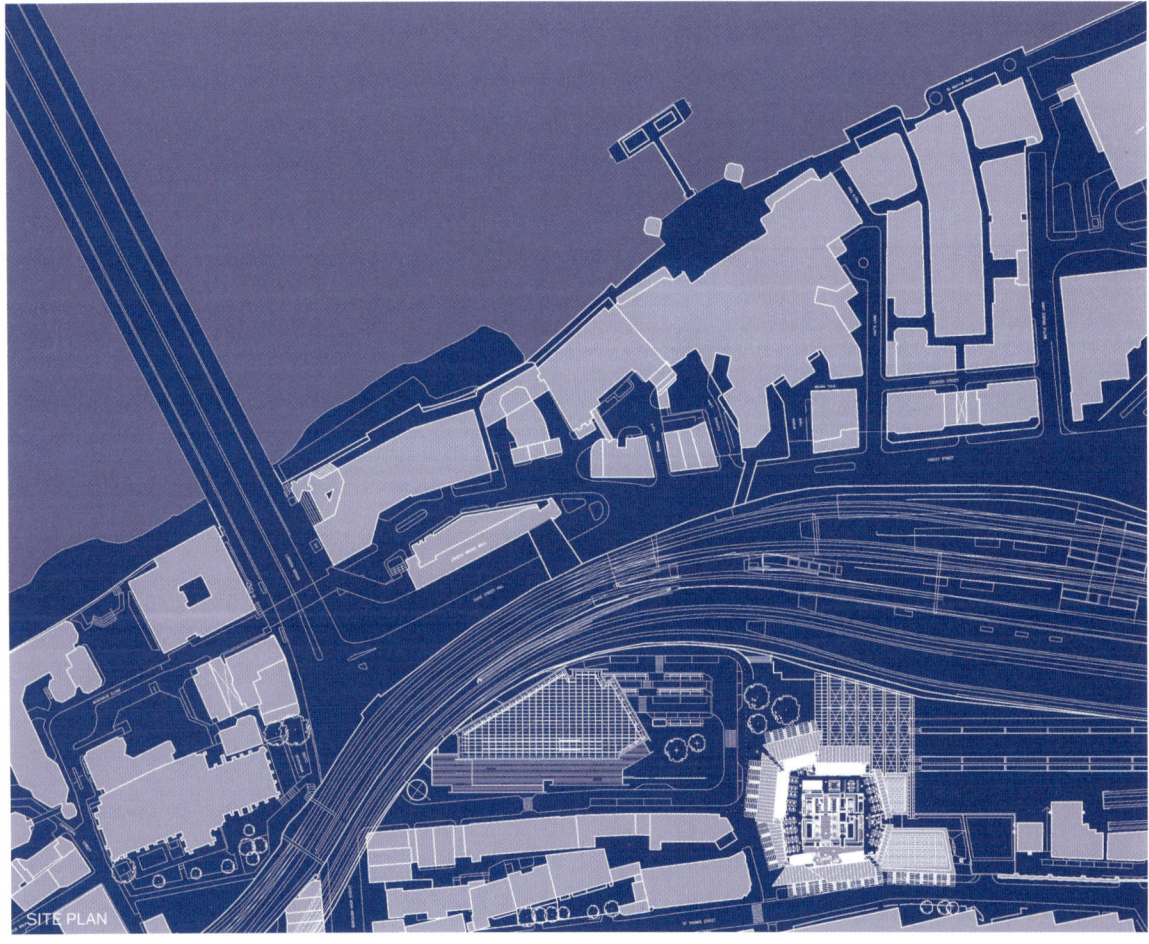
SITE PLAN

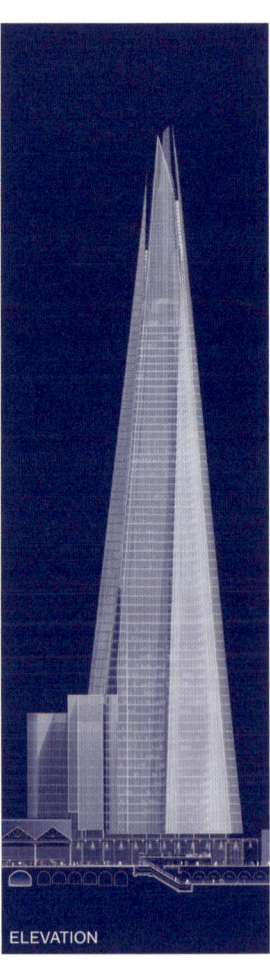
ELEVATION

Mixed Use

News Building

ARCHITECT RPBW Architects
DATE 2013
ADDRESS 3 London Bridge, SE1 9SG
CLIENT Sellar Property Group

views for swimmers. Above the hotel, on levels 53–65, luxury flats again have enviable views to the Thames estuary and Heathrow airport – weather permitting. The tower is topped by a public viewing gallery on levels 68–72. Above, the glazed façades rise another 61 metres to crown the building in spectacular fashion.

Next to the Shard and above London Bridge Underground station, the seventeen-storey News Building houses the global media and information company News UK, with 3,500 staff

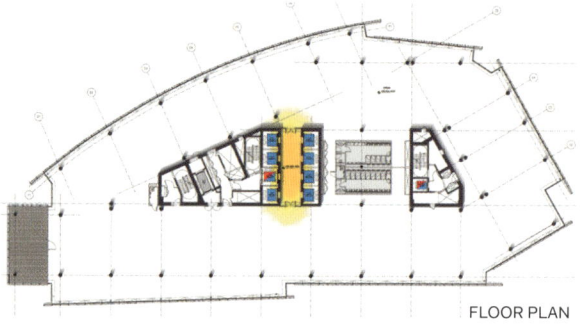

FLOOR PLAN

The group of buildings replaced two mundane office blocks near London Bridge station. The News Building has a sheer glazed façade that echoes that of the Shard itself.

ELEVATION

Mixed Use

Shard Place

ARCHITECT RPBW Architects
DATE Under construction
ADDRESS 28 London Bridge Street, SE1 9RY
CLIENT Sellar Property Group

working in the building. Its sheer, glazed form complements that of the Shard. Nearing completion is the third element in the scheme, Shard Place, a twenty-six-storey residential tower incorporating public and retail space, with an outdoor swimming pool at its summit.

Linked to the new London Bridge station, with Underground and mainline connections, the Shard Quarter is an intensive redevelopment on a 0.4-hectare site. The mix of uses it houses and the quality of its architecture, however, set it apart.

TYPICAL FLOOR PLAN

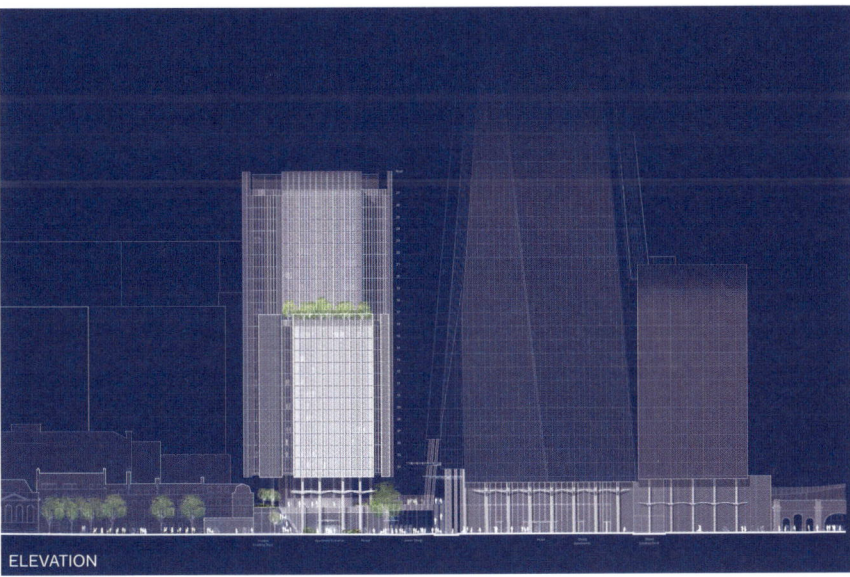

ELEVATION

Shard Place, the third of RPBW's projects at London Bridge, is a residential building with public and retail space at its base and a spectacular swimming pool at its summit.

Mixed Use

Education

New schools were a key element in the renewal of Britain after the Second World War, and Southwark's programme of school-building takes forward the spirit of the post-war era. At Phoenix Primary School in Bermondsey, John Pardey Architects successfully took on the task of expanding a listed school, an exemplar of progressive design from the 1960s, to accommodate a growing school roll and changing educational priorities. Rotherhithe Primary School occupied buildings from the 1970s, serving a large housing estate, which had aged so badly that demolition and replacement were the only option. Its RIBA Award-winning replacement capitalized on its one asset – a large tree-lined play area – to create 'a school in a garden' focused on a landscaped central space, and creating a new public face for the school, addressing the street and engaging with the community. A major initiative of Southwark Council has been the SEND programme, catering for pupils with special needs, addressed, for example, by Wright & Wright's Newlands Academy in Peckham. Provision for further and higher education has also been expanded significantly, with new buildings for London South Bank University, Southwark College and Camberwell College of Arts.

'The school is bright, airy and welcoming, teaching sustainability through its design – the best way to develop young citizens who respect and understand the environment by working and playing within it.'

STAFF MEMBER, ROTHERHITHE PRIMARY SCHOOL

ARK All Saints Academy, Highshore School and St Michael's Church

ARCHITECT Allford Hall Monaghan Morris
DATE 2014
ADDRESS 140 Wyndham Road, SE5 0UB
CLIENTS Balfour Beatty | London Borough of Southwark | ARK

ARK All Saints Academy and Highshore School occupy a site close to Camberwell New Road previously occupied by St Michael and All Angels Academy, a Church of England school. The old school, housed in a poor-quality 1970s building, closed after a long decline in standards, and the Ark Academy opened in 2013, catering for about 800 pupils aged between eleven and sixteen.

Located in a densely built-up urban quarter, the academy is a three-storey building facing directly on to Wyndham Road. The façade is formed of a brick base with aluminium cladding to the upper levels, punched through with windows. The entrance to the school is generous in scale, and welcoming. The ground floor houses shared facilities for the whole school: the reception area, administration, dining, the library and a lecture theatre. Teaching spaces, traditional classrooms and informal meeting rooms are on the two upper floors, clustered around internal courts and accessed via internal streets. The sports hall is a separate building, linked to generous external recreation spaces.

Highshore School, which serves pupils with special educational needs, is next to the academy. Entered via an open and welcoming entrance from Farmers Road, its internal plan, arranged around an atrium and internal courts, provides generous daylight and a clear sense of direction.

St Michael's church adjoins the academy on Wyndham Road. Although modest in scale, it has a striking steeple that makes it a local landmark. The calm, subtly daylit interior focuses on the cross-shaped window set in the south wall.

ARK All Saints Academy and Highshore School share a site (top). A separate sports hall is set in generous recreation spaces (left), while the attached church (above) is modest in scale but has a commanding street presence.

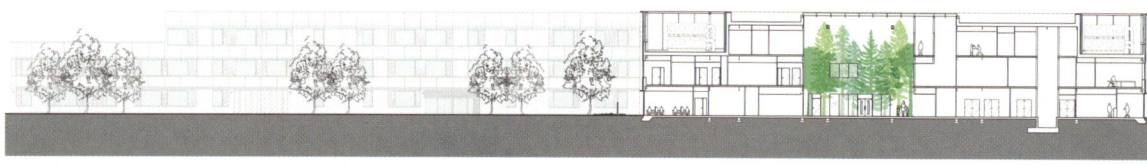

SECTION   ARK All Saints Academy (behind)   Highshore School

Rotherhithe Primary School

ARCHITECT Feilden Clegg Bradley Studios
DATE 2022
ADDRESS 61 Hawkstone Road, SE16 2PE
CLIENT London Borough of Southwark

Replacing a failed school building of the 1970s, and on a site where a school has stood for well over a century, Rotherhithe Primary School is a calm, elegant building, clad in carefully detailed brick and with a landscaped courtyard at its heart.

The site of Rotherhithe Primary, close to Southwark Park, has housed a school for 120 years. The last, completed in 1971, had reached the end of its life when a replacement was commissioned. Cold in winter, overheated in summer, it was nonetheless full of life and energy. The brief from Southwark was to enlarge the school intake as part of the council's ambitious primary-school expansion programme, with the constraint that the existing school was to stay open during construction and be demolished following the completion of its successor.

The school had one great asset: a large, tree-lined playground that provided space for learning, exploration and play and formed an oasis in a heavily built up area. Retaining and re-creating this space became a key objective of a landscape-led scheme for a 'school in a garden'. The new school would, like its predecessor, be a community asset, much in demand for local activities. The scheme pushed the public face of the school – the main entrance, foyer and assembly hall – to the edge of the site, addressing the surrounding area in a way that the existing building conspicuously failed to do and giving the new school a genuinely civic presence. The foyer hosts community events and displays the pupils' work.

Within the new school, a landscaped courtyard focused on a great red sycamore, surrounded by two storeys of classrooms, provides a calm space away from the busy streets. Older pupils have their base on the first floor, accessed via an external stair. Intimate spaces have been created for small group learning and sometimes play, and the seating areas created beneath the main staircase are particularly popular.

The exterior is clad in light brick on a concrete frame. The finely detailed form of the school, the architects suggest, echoes the history of an area in which shipbuilding was once a major employer. In its refined dignity, it has something of the austere poise of the warehouses of London's docks. The judges for the RIBA's 2024 regional awards were impressed by the degree to which 'the school motto, "hope and courage", has inspired the creation of a very special place of learning, with even its own construction seen as an educational opportunity.'

Bellenden Primary School

ARCHITECT Cottrell & Vermeulen
DATE 2018
ADDRESS Dewar Street, SE15 4JP
CLIENT London Borough of Southwark

On an island site surrounded by Victorian terraces, the dark brick responds to the context, while bold areas of colour emphasize the school's role as a beacon for the local community. Ground-floor classrooms for the early-years pupils open directly on to a central courtyard, with areas for both learning and play.

Replacing a 1970s primary school on a nearby site in Peckham Rye, Cottrell & Vermeulen's Bellenden Primary School occupies an island site enclosed on all sides by terraces of Victorian housing. The project, which is designed to accommodate an intake of 420 pupils plus 25 nursery places, was a response to increased demand for primary-school places in the borough. Its scale and materiality, with an extensive use of a dark-hued Belgian brick and clay tiles, relieved by the generous use of brightly coloured translucent polycarbonate panels, are a considered response to this context. The architects' aim was to make it a 'beacon' for the local community. The plan of the building – formed as a U-shape to enclose a central space, with areas for learning and for play – is far removed from the formal monumentality of London's Victorian schools. Covered spaces provide scope for outdoor learning in fine weather.

In the heart of London, pupils are provided with welcome access to open space. The courtyard at the heart of the school, flowing through to landscaped play areas and a formal games court, is surrounded by ground-floor classrooms for the youngest pupils, along with the assembly hall (which doubles as a dining hall), reception area, teachers' offices and the nursery. Most of the classrooms are on the first floor. Accessed by external stairs, each of which serves a pair of classrooms, some of them open on to external learning terraces. Corridors are kept to a minimum, and the ground-floor classrooms are accessed via the playground. Cottrell & Vermeulen's architecture evokes distinct memories of the early post-war schools: rejecting earnestness in favour of a playful aesthetic that reflects the aims of the school.

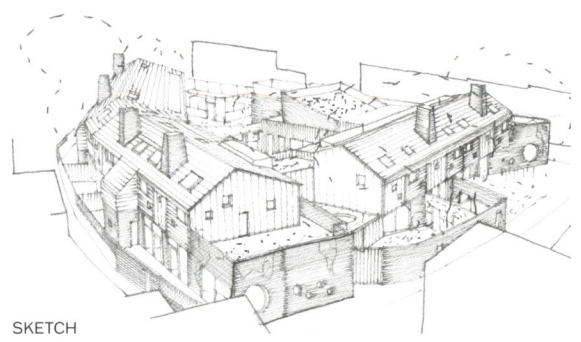

SKETCH

Education

SILS3 Pupil Referral Unit

ARCHITECT Tim Ronalds Architects
DATE 2021
ADDRESS 2 Davey Street, SE16 6LF
CLIENT London Borough of Southwark

SILS3 (Southwark Inclusive Learning Service Key Stage 3) is a school with an agenda: to reintegrate into the educational system pupils excluded from mainstream schools on account of behavioural or emotional problems. Formally described as a pupil referral unit, it caters for a small number of pupils aged between eleven and fourteen, taught in small classes by specialist teachers.

The site is close to an existing facility housed inadequately in a building that had once been a residential children's home (this was subsequently demolished). The architects describe the brief as for 'a calm, secure and robust educational environment that would improve the life chances of the children'. Research into the specific needs addressed by the school generated a building that is cheerful, optimistic and far removed from the defensive ethos that formerly pervaded 'special' schools. Internally, it is open and generously scaled, with wide corridors and open vistas leaving no hidden areas that can generate bad behaviour. The fit-out is of high quality – no institutional parsimony here – with oak floors, maple joinery and pine-faced acoustic ceilings. The open, welcoming aesthetic of the architecture is expressed externally in façades of white brick with large 'picture' windows, those on the first floor looking out to Burgess Park (page 142). There is no sense of enclosure, although the architecture provides security along with friendliness and calm. The school's robust construction and high-quality materials – it was built to a traditional contract, rather than design-and-build – make it highly sustainable.

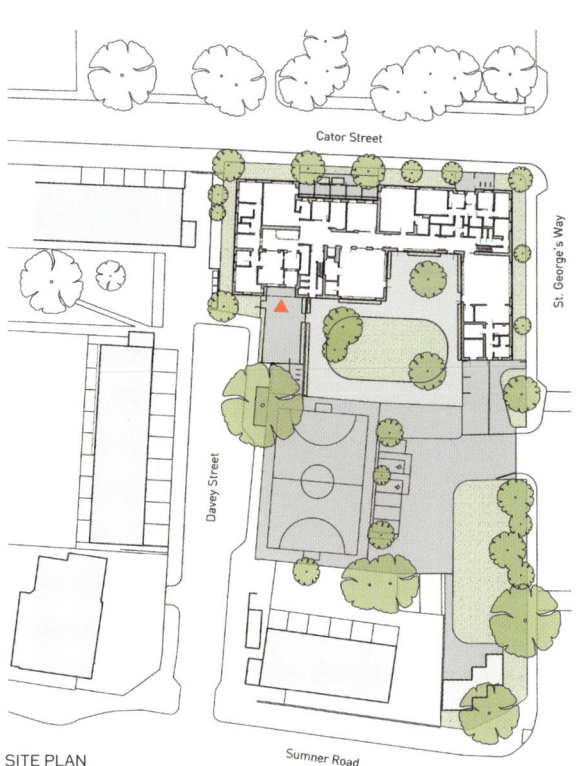

SITE PLAN

The unit provides its pupils with a secure environment that nevertheless brings no sense of enclosure or confinement, with ample outside space and calming views over the adjacent park.

Education

Cherry Garden School

ARCHITECT Hawkins\Brown
DATE 2019
ADDRESS 41 Bellenden Road, SE15 5BB
CLIENT London Borough of Southwark

Cherry Garden School was commissioned in response to Southwark Council's SEND (Special Educational Needs or Disabilities) programme, designed to address the special needs of children with learning differences and autism. It was based in Bermondsey before its relocation to Peckham, where the new school building caters for just seventy-five pupils, plus a ten-place nursery and satellite class.

The building is designed in response to a very specific brief, reflecting the need for individualized learning and support that is fundamental to its mission. A double-height hub, expressed as a lightweight element linking two accommodation blocks – brick-clad in deference to the character of the surrounding streets – forms the heart of the building, housing specialist but adaptable teaching spaces. Classrooms are on the perimeter, generously daylit and open in character. The approach of the school is holistic, and a play terrace, soft playrooms and a hydrotherapy pool are an important element of the school's strategy.

NORTH ELEVATION

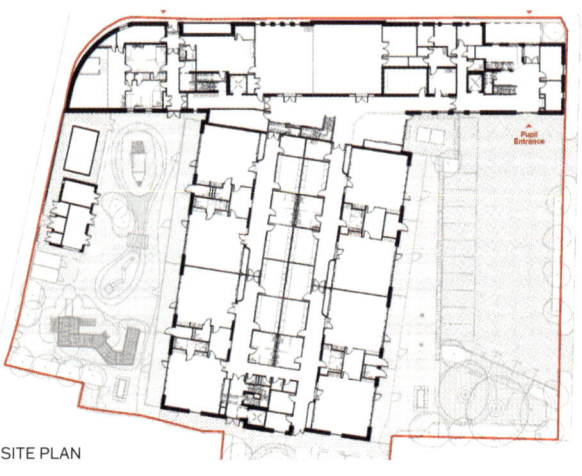

SITE PLAN

Cherry Garden School caters for pupils with special needs, with a double-height hub of teaching spaces at its heart and classrooms at the outer edges. Landscaped play areas and gardens form the setting for the brick-clad building, which is simultaneously secure and welcoming.

Newlands Academy

ARCHITECT Wright & Wright
DATE 2013
ADDRESS Stuart Road, SE15 3AZ
CLIENTS 4Futures | London Borough of Southwark

NORTH ELEVATION

The architecture addresses the requirement for a secure environment, but the emphasis of the school – expressed in the buildings – is on equipping young people to reintegrate into society.

Newlands Academy in Peckham is another product of the SEND initiative, catering for seventy boys, aged between eleven and sixteen, with serious behavioural or emotional problems. Some have been convicted of serious crimes, others have been the victims of crime, while yet others are hyperactive or seriously withdrawn. Traditionally, many would have been subjected to a Borstal-style environment little better than imprisonment.

In designing Newlands, the architects had to address serious questions of security. The building deals with these discreetly; an 'outreach' entrance point, for example, provides for the occasions when pupils may need to be interviewed by police or probation officers. Gates on corridors allow effective lockdown in the event of serious disturbance, but the emphasis of the school – expressed in the architecture, from the friendly, well-crafted brick exterior inwards – is on providing pupils with an education that will offer them a better future and integrate them with the wider world.

The facilities are those of any well-equipped secondary school. Drama, for example, is an important part of the curriculum, and the well-equipped auditorium can be extended into the courtyard in fine weather. The school interior has a generosity in scale and detail that is totally at odds with the ethos of an 'institution'. A broad 'street' runs through the building, offering views through the interior and constituting a key ingredient in the agenda of openness; compartmentalization would have been at odds with that. Working to a very tight budget, the architects – who cite the Finnish architect Alvar Aalto and the Swedish Sigurd Lewerentz as inspiration – have created a building that is clearly in a great tradition of public architecture.

Phoenix Primary School

ARCHITECTS John Pardey Architects | HKR Architects
DATE 2010
ADDRESS Marlborough Grove, SE1 5JT
CLIENT London Borough of Southwark

Phoenix Primary School in Bermondsey opened in 1967 as Eveline Lowe School, named after a notable socialist politician and sometime chair of London County Council. Replacing a Blitzed Victorian school, it was designed by the practice of David and Mary Medd (best known for their work on the Hertfordshire schools programme) and listed Grade II in 2006 as 'a rather outstanding success of educational philosophy-driven design'. Its low-rise form, with teaching spaces in single-storey brick pavilions opening on to a central garden, was deliberate, since most of the pupils lived in high-rise blocks of flats. Retaining the landscape setting was a key objective of the scheme; it provided 'a place of retreat and a theatre of interaction for children of different age groups and their teachers'.

The competition-winning scheme for the expansion of the school in 2007 addressed the need to accommodate 420 pupils plus a nursery unit for 50 children. Designed with Sir Colin Stansfield Smith as consultant and with the support of David Medd, it reflected the architects' respect for the existing building but addressed its shortcomings, notably the inadequate scale (by twenty-first-century standards) of its classrooms and the degraded state of much of the surrounding site, which was given over to car parking.

The street-facing parking area provided the site for new buildings, while the rear playground was left untouched. 'A necklace of new buildings', two storeys high and contrasting in materials with the 1960s brick and tiles, was placed along the street elevations. The existing classrooms were repurposed as 'resource spaces', but left untouched. A key aim was to retain them as distinct elements, maintaining a clear division between the listed buildings and the additions. The new classrooms, set off corridors, are far removed from the Medds' radical vision, but with windows opening to the playground, they reflect twenty-first-century approaches to teaching.

ELEVATION

Phoenix Primary School, unlike many others of the 1960s, has weathered well. The retention of its landscaped setting was a priority in a project that has married the 1960s to the twenty-first century.

Spa School

ARCHITECT AOC
DATE 2011
ADDRESS Monnow Road, SE1 5RN
CLIENT London Borough of Southwark

The new structure, adjacent to the school's main (Victorian) building (bottom right), takes inspiration both from its neighbour and, more exotically, from 'visual signs and material presence'. There is a clear strand of Post-modernism in its form and detailing, the architects having the courage to reject narrow modernist prescriptions.

AOC's new building for Spa School provides a striking contrast – superficially at least – to the general character of new school design in Southwark. It forms an addition to an established school in a Conservation Area in Bermondsey, catering specifically for pupils aged between eleven and nineteen and affected by autism. The external form of the building reflects the concerns of a practice, still youthful, that is 'interested in how architecture can communicate through both visual signs and material presence' but, for all the exuberance of its work, is reluctant to accept a Post-modernist label. The building was designed in the context of a masterplan commissioned from AOC for the school site, and occupies a previously undeveloped gap site.

The gabled roofline of the existing school building – a classic Victorian board school – clearly provided inspiration for AOC's tri-gabled street elevation, executed in hard modern brick and relieved by a pattern of brick crosses. The use of polychromy is not confined to the exterior of the building; inside, colourful tiling is a feature and a staircase is formed of metal with almost Art Nouveau wilfulness. The stair, rising through a top-lit circulation space, forms the centre of the plan, allowing access to six classrooms on two levels.

GROUND-FLOOR PLAN

Dulwich College Laboratory

ARCHITECT Grimshaw
DATE 2016
ADDRESS Dulwich Common, SE21 7LD
CLIENT Dulwich College

Dulwich College, founded in the early seventeenth century, moved into a new, imposing complex designed by Charles Barry Jr in the 1860s. The growth of the college has since generated many additional buildings on its leafy campus. The latest is the Laboratory, a major addition, housing twenty-one laboratories, exhibition spaces and an auditorium, and seen as a 'home for science and a venue for the arts'. The site, close to the main college building, was that of an undistinguished, poor-quality 1950s building that made no attempt to relate to its context and was highly inefficient in terms of its energy demands.

The college's brief called for an efficient and economical building, 'built to last' and capable of adaptation to the teaching needs of the future. It should also be highly sustainable in tune with the college's wider sustainability strategy, and this objective was a major driver of the project. The teaching spaces in the S-shaped building face east, west and north. The plant room supplies heat not only to the Laboratory but also to the main college building. Visors fitted to the windows baffle solar gain, and cooling is supplied via a thermally active building system (TABS), an economical alternative to conventional air conditioning that uses an 'open loop' system to channel groundwater through ceilings and soffits to extract heat. Photovoltaic panels are fitted to roofs, further reducing the energy demands of the building, and its energy performance is made visible to all users via a performance 'dashboard' on screens throughout the communal areas.

Teaching and laboratory spaces are arranged around two communal areas, with the biology, physics and chemistry departments each having a floor of the building. A timber-panelled atrium, the James Caird Hall, proudly displays the lifeboat of explorer Ernest Shackleton, a Dulwich alumnus. A multipurpose 240-seat auditorium can be adapted for theatrical and musical performances, lectures and other events, and – since the college sees itself as part of the wider community – is made available to local groups.

The building's embrace of the arts and sciences is symbolized by the ceramic façade designed by the sculptor Peter Randall-Page RA (who had previously worked with Grimshaw on the Eden Project in Cornwall), working in collaboration with a group of pupils from the college. Based on the system developed by the Hungarian biologist Aristid Lindenmayer to explain the growth of plants, the system is expressed on two façades of the building, including in vivid colour on a west-facing wall, where it is strikingly illuminated by the setting sun. Commitment to the intersection of arts and sciences is further illustrated by a hanging sculpture by Conrad Shawcross RA, again the product of a fruitful collaboration with pupils at the college.

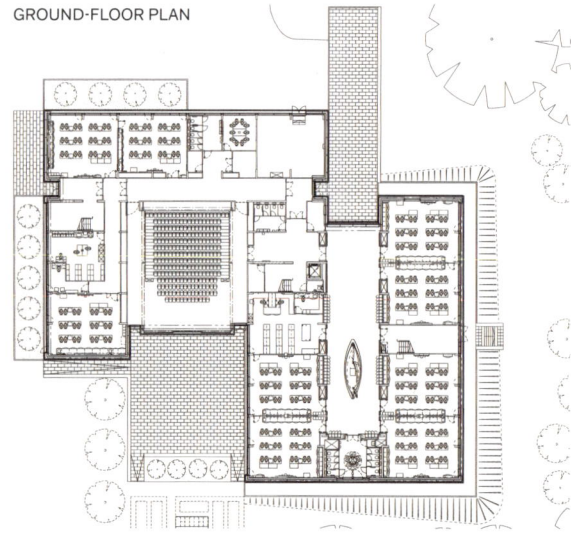

GROUND-FLOOR PLAN

Laboratories, exhibition spaces and an auditorium are housed in a building – enriched with several major art commissions – that reflects the breadth of teaching in the school. The ceramic façade (below) was designed by Peter Randall-Page RA in collaboration with pupils.

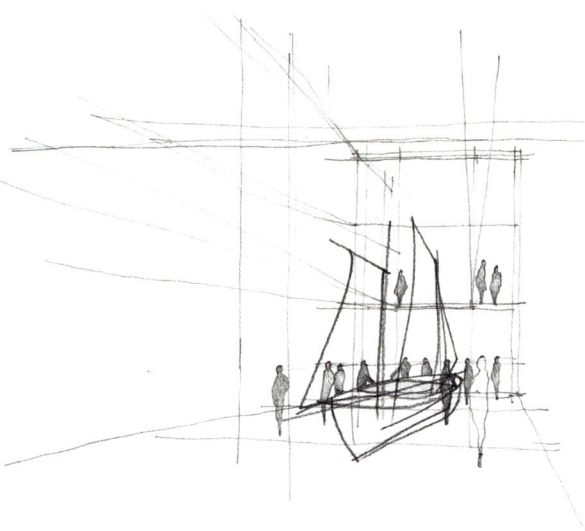

INTERIOR SKETCH

Education

Haberdashers' Borough Academy

ARCHITECTS Collado Collins | PTAL
DATE 2023
ADDRESS 94B Southwark Bridge Road, SE1 0EX
CLIENT Hadston Southwark Ltd

The site for this project has great historic interest as the former headquarters of the Metropolitan Fire Brigade (established 1865). It incorporates the former 1770s workhouse known as Winchester House, used by the brigade as its headquarters and training centre, as well as major additions completed in 1878 and 1911. A further late Victorian building on Southwark Bridge Road was demolished in the 1960s. By 2014 the site had been completely vacated after a period of run-down, leaving the Grade II-listed buildings vacant.

Collado Collins' development of the fire station site was based on an intensive study of its history, which formed the basis for planning and listed-building applications, during the course of which many inappropriate later structures were identified for removal. The redevelopment of the site, close to Borough Underground station, created a major new

The listed complex, including the late eighteenth-century Winchester House (opposite) and notable Victorian additions, has been reimagined with sympathetic new buildings.

school, catering initially for 700 pupils aged between sixteen and eighteen, designed by PTAL and incorporating the listed Winchester House. (Sports facilities for the school, including a hall and pitches, were created on a neighbouring area of land known as the Grotto thanks to an earlier pleasure garden and spa on the site.)

The listed fire-station buildings were converted for residential use, providing 199 new units. This has produced a highly successful combination of old and new, with a new ten-storey residential building skilfully slotted into the southwest portion of the site, which focuses on a landscaped courtyard.

Education

Clarence Centre for Enterprise and Innovation, LSBU

ARCHITECT Rivington Street Studio
DATE 2014
ADDRESS 6 St George's Circus, SE1 6LF
CLIENT London South Bank University

The Clarence Centre for Enterprise and Innovation, founded by London South Bank University, is designed to support young entrepreneurs (many of them LSBU graduates) by providing workspaces along with a gallery, a café and other support facilities. The project occupies a group of Georgian terraced houses, plus a pub, close to the university's Southwark campus. Long derelict and disused, the seventeen houses – the last surviving section of St George's Circus, and now standing within the St George's Circus Conservation Area designated by Southwark Council – had faced demolition to make way for a university development, but were listed Grade II in 2000. Their listed status provided a challenge for the architects charged with refashioning them as twenty-first-century educational spaces.

The £13 million project created a unique new 2,900-square-metre facility for the university. The challenge was to obtain listed-building consent, respecting the historic character of the buildings and updating them

LONDON ROAD: FRONT ELEVATION

LONDON ROAD: REAR ELEVATION

in line with current environmental criteria. Derelict additions were removed as part of a stage of consolidating the buildings, and floors and roofs were strengthened. Natural ventilation with opening windows was the strategy for much of the complex, and in some areas passive cooling was used, circulating cool air from basement areas through a network of ducts. Photovoltaic panels on some roof areas supplement the energy needs of the centre, and modern glazing and insulation limit heat loss. Full disabled access was a fundamental objective, with lift access to all levels.

As part of a project that combines faithful restoration with innovative intervention, surviving shopfronts were retained and repaired to retain the familiar street scene. New accommodation was wrapped around the back of the terraces, creating a central courtyard. The principal point of entry to the complex is through the former Duke of Clarence pub, an illustration of the project's marriage of old and new to meet present-day needs.

The project rescued a group of listed, but derelict and disused, Georgian houses that were part of the historic St George's Circus development. The project included the restoration of the old buildings and the addition of new space around a courtyard.

Education 123

LSBU Hub

ARCHITECT WilkinsonEyre
DATE 2022
ADDRESS London Road, SE1 6NJ
CLIENT London South Bank University

London South Bank University's London Road Building was a prominent, if rather forbidding, landmark on the major road close to Elephant and Castle. Completed in 1976, it presented a blank elevation to the street and internally was confused and institutional in character. Its services needed renewal and its thermal performance was poor. It was, however, the largest building on LSBU's main campus, containing 20 per cent of the university's space for teaching and learning.

WilkinsonEyre's project, characterized as a 'deep renovation', transformed this problematic building into an impressive centrepiece of the campus, housing the university library, study rooms, lecture theatres, digital suites and meeting rooms over an area of more than 20,000 square metres. Non-academic spaces include a food court, a coffee shop, an exhibition space and a gymnasium for the university's Academy of Sport. The existing concrete structure was largely retained, its hostile brick façades replaced with permeable glazed frontages opening up the building to the wider community. A car park to the southeast was transformed into an attractive new square, and the main entrance to the building leads into a column-free atrium, an impressive and

In a remarkable transformation, an unloved 1970s building that housed a significant part of the university's teaching and learning space has become a worthy centrepiece for the campus.

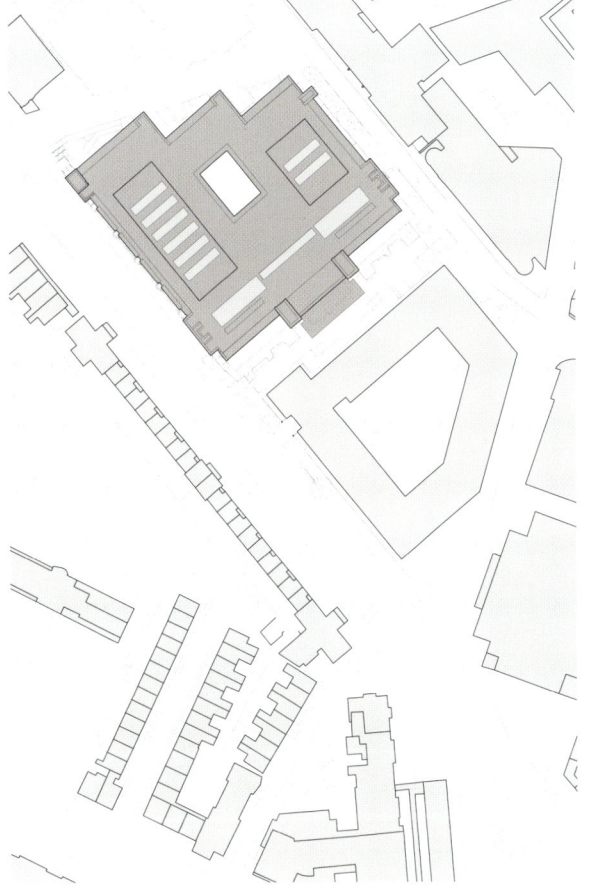

GROUND-FLOOR PLAN

ELEVATION

Education

Education

inviting space that forms the heart of the Hub. From there, a broad staircase ascends to the upper-ground-floor concourse – although new lift provision guarantees access for all.

The most remarkable space in the building is the library, a truly spectacular interior, with floors hung from steel roof beams, removing the need for internal columns and foundations. It contains a variety of study spaces and is filled with controlled natural light.

The building's location, in a densely built-up area close to heavily trafficked roads, ruled out a natural ventilation strategy in most internal spaces. Instead, demand-control mechanical ventilation is the general strategy. Façades have been designed to limit solar gain, while the retention of most of the 1970s structure allowed savings of up to 50 per cent of embodied carbon. The completed building achieved a Very Good BREEAM rating.

The building contains teaching spaces and student facilities, including a spectacular library.

Education

Southwark College

ARCHITECTS GTH Architects | Platform 5 Architects
DATE 2015–17
ADDRESS 25 The Cut, SE1 8DF
CLIENT NCG Group

NORTH ELEVATION

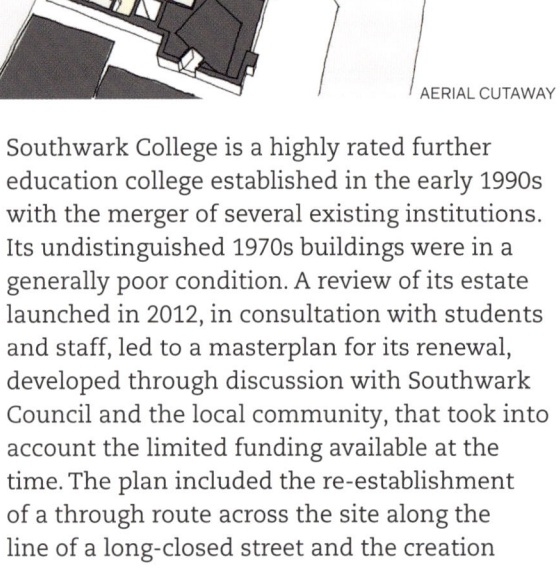

AERIAL CUTAWAY

Southwark College is a highly rated further education college established in the early 1990s with the merger of several existing institutions. Its undistinguished 1970s buildings were in a generally poor condition. A review of its estate launched in 2012, in consultation with students and staff, led to a masterplan for its renewal, developed through discussion with Southwark Council and the local community, that took into account the limited funding available at the time. The plan included the re-establishment of a through route across the site along the line of a long-closed street and the creation of a new public pocket park, a precious asset in a densely built-up area.

The project was led by GTH Architects in collaboration with Platform 5 Architects. The first phase of the renewal, which was constrained by the scarcity of funding, focused on the refurbishment of the 1970s block on The Cut. Carried out in 2015, it offered a more accessible entrance for the college and a reception area leading to the impressive new central atrium, the heart of the college, containing a landmark spiral staircase – painted bright red – flexible learning spaces and a café, all set under a sawtooth roof that channels in generous yet controlled daylight. The renewed building mediates in scale and materials between the low-rise Young Vic and the highly expressive Palestra building,

designed by the late Will Alsop, at the junction with Blackfriars Road.

The second phase of the project, which opened in 2017, created 7,500 square metres of new space for the college, demolishing the existing, largely two-storey buildings and replacing them with blocks of between five and seven storeys housing specialist departments, including dance, drama, music, digital media and science laboratories. The buildings wrap around the atrium, highlighting the themes of transparent learning, participation and community that are central to the college's work. The entire – radical – renewal of the site took place without interrupting its teaching.

The 1970s building was radically renewed, with a striking atrium (above) focusing on a dramatic red staircase (opposite, right) and teaching/recreation spaces under a roof that floods the space with light.

Education

Camberwell College of Arts

ARCHITECT Stephen Marshall Architects
DATE 2017
ADDRESS 45–65 Peckham Road, SE5 8UF
CLIENT University of the Arts London

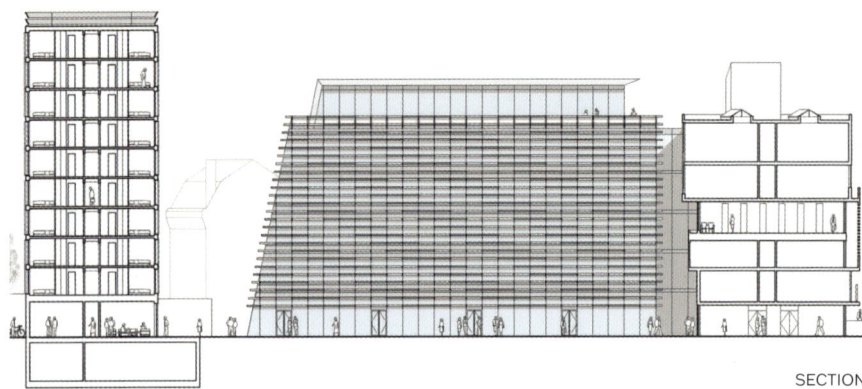
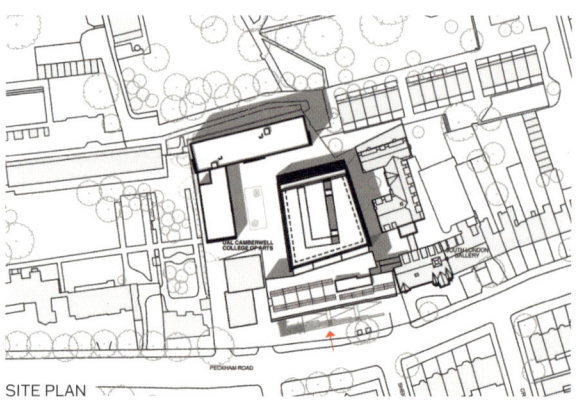

SECTION SITE PLAN

Established as the Camberwell School of Arts and Crafts in 1898, Camberwell College is now a constituent college of the University of the Arts London (UAL). It occupies a series of buildings along Peckham Road, the earliest of which was designed by Maurice Bingham Adams in 1897 and is now partly occupied by the South London Gallery. The 1960s building designed by Murray, Ward & Partners – described in *The Buildings of England* as 'totally unsympathetic' – was in poor condition, with concrete spalling. Access was at first-floor level, via an external staircase.

The brief called for the provision of 264 student rooms and 6,500 square metres of teaching space, with disabled access throughout, and new external landscaping. The new brick-clad student housing is contained in an L-shaped block around a courtyard closed at one end by the 1890s building. The new teaching building is a dramatic composition,

Education

clad with a glazing system that incorporates solar shading designed to ensure the provision of controlled daylight to the studio spaces. It also houses the college's library, the student canteen and a large lecture theatre. The 1960s building was radically refurbished, in sympathy with the original designs, to address problems of structure and access, and the decayed concrete addressed by specialist contractors.

The interior design of the new teaching block and the refurbished 1960s building was undertaken by Stephen Marshall Architects (the practice also responsible for new student accommodation buildings for UAL in Peckham, completed in 2023). Furniture for the Camberwell project, including the angled stacks of the library, is by Ab Rogers Design.

The 1960s block was radically refurbished (opposite and above), making it more accessible and tackling its decaying structure.

A new teaching building clad in an innovative glazing system is a dramatic addition, while a brick-clad block houses 264 students (top).

Education

Landscape

The old image of Southwark as 'a desert of red brick' hardly applies to a borough that has been transformed by new parks and public spaces during the process of regeneration and renewal. Elephant Park, created as part of the transformation of the former Heygate estate site, has at its heart the Tree House, an award-winning project by Bell Phillips hailed as 'a civic presence in the park'. Burgess Park in Camberwell was created after much of its site was cleared by wartime bombing, but became run-down and crime-ridden. It has been re-created to great effect, its lake cleared of rubbish and vegetation, redundant roads removed and a canal drained, and landscaping and tree-planting transforming it into a heavily used and welcoming amenity. More modest public spaces have been created as a by-product of new developments across Southwark. One of the first results of the redevelopment of the Aylesbury estate was the creation of a new square, and indeed squares and gardens are elements of most recent housing schemes in Southwark; the masterplan for Canada Water includes the creation of a new park, introducing generous open space into an area that conspicuously lacked it.

'It's a great city park, vibrant and diverse. It feels as though the whole world is represented here and can find their own spot.'

A BURGESS PARK LOCAL

Elephant Park

SITE PLAN

The Heygate estate (1970–74) contained 1,212 homes in unsatisfactory deck-access blocks. Phased demolition was completed in 2014, and a masterplan for the site commissioned by developer Lendlease. Construction will extend to 2030. Elephant Park, as the new urban quarter is known, will provide more than 2,500 new homes – 25 per cent of them classed as affordable – as well as shops, offices, restaurants, community facilities and open spaces. This lively new district is a key element in the renewal of Elephant and Castle.

At the heart of the development is a new 0.8-hectare public park. At its centre, in turn, is the Tree House by Bell Phillips, a twenty-first-century version of the follies built for the owners of Georgian country estates. But this one is designed for use by everyone. Constructed around a mature plane tree, it incorporates a café, an internal community space (which can be opened to the park in fine weather) and

Allford Hall Monaghan Morris's contribution (opposite and this page) includes three phases of development, providing a mix of high-rise and mansion blocks set among generous public spaces.

Landscape

The Tree House

ARCHITECT Bell Phillips
DATE 2021
ADDRESS Deacon Street/Sayer Street, SE17 1GD
CLIENT Lendlease

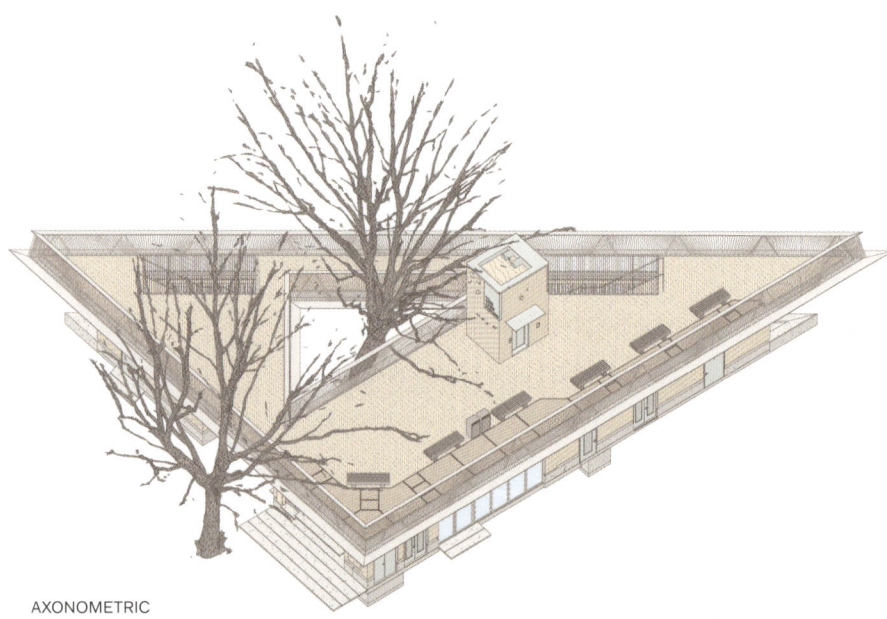

AXONOMETRIC

a rooftop terrace. 'Touch the ground lightly' was the guiding principle, so construction is lightweight. With a structure of cross-laminated timber (rather than steel or concrete), timber cladding and a bamboo floor, the building is designed to celebrate and be part of its setting. It won an RIBA Regional Award in 2024, the judges praising its 'civic presence' and finding it 'a joy and a relief to see a building of this scale in the heart of such a dense … development'.

The first element (completed in 2015) of the Heygate masterplan was Trafalgar Place, a development of 235 homes, 25 per cent designated 'affordable', designed by dRMM with Grant Associates as landscape architect. Focused on a new, generously planted

The Tree House is a twenty-first-century – lightweight – version of the Georgian garden pavilion, for the enjoyment of all.

Landscape 137

Trafalgar Place

ARCHITECT dRMM
DATE 2015
ADDRESS Rodney Road, SE17 1AS
CLIENT Lendlease

SITE PLAN

pedestrian street, with an internal courtyard for the use of residents, the development contains blocks of between four and ten storeys, plus a landmark tower. The plan also retained twenty-five mature trees on the site.

Maccreanor Lavington's South Gardens scheme provides 360 homes on a site planned as three plots connected by a landscaped, tree-lined public realm. The project includes twenty-eight terraced houses, mansion blocks of between seven and ten storeys – a virtuoso revival of a traditional format – and a single sixteen-storey tower. The concrete-framed housing uses a variety of brick, carefully detailed, as cladding, and bay windows refer

The Trafalgar Place development (this page) consists of a mix of terraced houses and mansion blocks with a single sixteen-storey tower, all set in a landscaped public realm with extensive tree planting.

South Gardens

ARCHITECT Maccreanor Lavington
DATE 2017
ADDRESS Heygate Street, SE17 1FP
CLIENT Lendlease

subtly to Victorian traditions. A terrace of fifteen houses has cross-laminated timber as part of an ultra-low-energy strategy that has achieved Passivhaus accreditation.

Allford Hall Monaghan Morris is responsible for three projects forming part of Elephant Park, all of which feature a mix of high-rise and lower blocks of eight to twelve storeys with the scale of the traditional London mansion block, integrating retail and amenity spaces. Park Central West was the first to be completed, focused on a twenty-four-storey tower. The second phase, West Grove, includes the tallest building in the masterplan: 31 storeys with 222 homes. A ten-storey building at the junction of Heygate Street and Walworth Road mediates with the scale of the surrounding area. The final phase, Park Central East, addressing New Kent Road, includes five buildings, with 384 homes of a mix of tenures, linked by a single-storey podium containing shops and other amenities.

Maccreanor Lavington's work at Elephant Park (this page) consists of 360 homes in a series of formats that reflect the character of the surrounding area while addressing present-day housing needs.

Landscape

Canada Water Masterplan

ARCHITECTS Allies and Morrison | Hawkins\Brown | Townshend Landscape Architects
DATE Under construction
ADDRESS Canada Water, SE16
CLIENT British Land

Surrey Docks, developed from the early eighteenth century onwards on the Rotherhithe peninsula, were the centre of Britain's timber-importing trade. But by 1970 they were entirely closed and large areas infilled. The former Canada Dock (opened 1876) was refashioned as Canada Water, and the 1980s and 90s brought the construction of public housing, a large shopping centre, a retail park and a printing works. The area's relative isolation was rectified in 1999 with the opening of Canada Water Jubilee line station, providing a direct link to the West End and Canary Wharf. More recently the station has been connected by the London Overground, which also serves Surrey Quays station.

The Canada Water masterplan, commissioned by British Land and being implemented with its joint-venture partner AustralianSuper, covers an area of 21.5 hectares between Canada Water and the former Greenland Dock. It provides for 3,000 new homes, 185,800 square metres of workspace, and 93,000 square metres of retail, leisure and community space, as well as 6.5 hectares – a third of the total site – of parks and open spaces. The old shopping centre will be demolished and replaced with a new 'high street' and town square linking the two stations. The former printing works (which found an interim use as a live music venue) will, on completion in 2027 to designs by Hawkins\Brown, be a spectacular

MASTERPLAN

The transformation of the docks includes the spectacular cultural buildings Printworks London and the Grand Press (below left and bottom), and a project to turn the former Canada Dock into an asset for people and for nature (below), as well as residential development.

cultural space as Printworks London, alongside 14,700 square metres of workspace to be known as the Grand Press. New pedestrian and cycle routes and open spaces will include a 1.4-hectare park, part of a public-space masterplan by Townshend Landscape Architects. Townshend's scheme includes the major restoration of Canada Dock (a designated Site of Importance for Nature Conservation) in collaboration with London Wildlife Trust, creating a haven for wildlife and making special provision for nesting birds.

As part of the masterplan, Allies and Morrison has been commissioned to design two new buildings close to Canada Water station. The first, The Founding, provides thirty-five storeys of housing above a five-storey podium containing workspaces and shops. The second, Dock Shed, contains 21,200 square metres of workspaces as well as a leisure centre containing two swimming pools, gym and squash courts, with a large, daylit staircase at its centre.

Burgess Park

ARCHITECTS LDA Design | Bell Phillips
DATE 2012–24
ADDRESS Albany Road/St George's Way, SE5 0AL
CLIENT London Borough of Southwark

Burgess Park in Camberwell is, at 56 hectares, one of the largest public parks in south London. It was a product of the intensive bombing of the surrounding area during the Second World War, and the idea of a park was promoted in Patrick Abercrombie's *Greater London Plan* of 1944, which placed emphasis on the necessity for new open spaces in heavily built-up inner London.

The creation of the park, over a number of years, was the achievement of London County Council, succeeded by the Greater London Council, assembling land cleared by bombing and by slum clearance but in the absence of a coherent plan. By the time a competition – won by LDA in 2009 – was launched for a radical re-creation of the park, it was run-down and crime-ridden. A basic element of LDA's scheme, involving intensive consultation with the local community, was the creation of

Created after the area was devastated by wartime bombs, Burgess Park became a major asset for south London, but had deteriorated. Its re-creation has made it an amenity for local people of all ages.

a more legible structure for the park, with clear sight lines. Redundant roads were removed, the derelict Grand Surrey Canal filled in and a new network of paths laid out; the lake was cleared of debris and vegetation, and reworked. A new playground, a competition-standard BMX track, a landscaped meadow designed by the celebrated ecological designer James Hitchmough, a new café and extensive tree-planting transformed the park.

More recently, Burgess Park West – long regarded as an unsafe area – has undergone a similar transformation, with a flagship children's playground and the launch of Burgess Sports. The new sports hub, designed by Bell Phillips and completed in 2024, is a flexible, durable building containing changing rooms, a club room, staff offices and public amenities. New sports pitches and a ball court have been completed and a skate bowl, one of the largest skate parks in Europe, is planned.

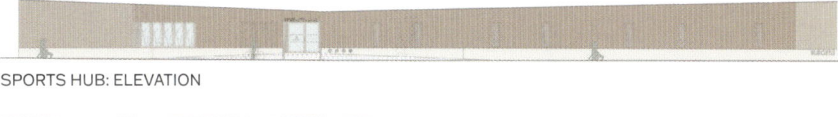

SPORTS HUB: ELEVATION

Landscape

One Tower Bridge and Potters Fields Park

Potters Fields Park – named after the industry that flourished there in the seventeenth century – was opened in 1988 on the site of former dock warehouses destroyed by Second World War bombing. A major relandscaping scheme was completed in 2007. Southwark Council owned the site of the One Tower Bridge development, adjacent to the park, until 2001, when it was acquired by Berkeley Homes. Following a planning inquiry, consent was subsequently obtained for a housing scheme featuring eight cylindrical towers, designed by Ian Ritchie Architects. This scheme, which was supported by the Commission for Architecture and the Built Environment but strongly opposed by local residents, was abandoned in 2008 in favour of a new project by Squire & Partners, designed to capitalize on the site's proximity to Tower Bridge.

A key feature is a single, slender tower, conceived as a campanile, twenty storeys in height, with just one flat per floor. Clad in Gris Catalan limestone, with anodized bronze windows, the tower acts as an elegant marker for the development. Three blocks, using a similar vocabulary of materials, occupy the central portion of the site. Two further blocks, stepping down in scale towards Tower Bridge Road, are clad in London stock brick, with projecting balconies. (Near the junction of Tower Bridge Road and Tooley Street the LaLiT hotel, a conversion of E.W. Mountford's 1890s Grade II-listed South London College, makes exemplary use of brick.) A new pedestrian route, Duchess Walk, extends from Queen Elizabeth Street towards the Bridge Theatre (see pages 14–15) and is lined with shops and restaurants.

SKETCH

The project is a vigorous but respectful neighbour to Tower Bridge, consisting of a single high-rise block (opposite, top left) and lower blocks around Potters Fields Park (opposite, bottom).

Landscape

ARCHITECT Squire & Partners
DATE 2017
ADDRESS Tooley Street/Tower Bridge Road, SE1 2UD
CLIENT Berkeley Homes

Landscape

145

Dickens' Fields

ARCHITECT LDA Design
DATE 2021
ADDRESS Falmouth Road/Harper Road, SE1 4JL
CLIENT London Borough of Southwark

In 2014 Southwark Council committed £1 million to regenerate Dickens' Fields and nearby open spaces as part of a package of improvements for public areas around Elephant and Castle. Located between the Rockingham estate and Trinity Church Square, Dickens' Fields was created on land cleared as the result of a V2 rocket strike during the Second World War. It is a precious open space in a densely built-up part of the borough.

LDA Design worked for several years on the development of the project to improve the space as a local amenity. Meetings with the local community produced ideas that fed into a scheme to make Dickens' Fields welcoming, biodiverse and accessible to all. Dickens' Square Road was closed and integrated into the park. Entrances on Harper Road and Brockham Street were transformed, with walls removed to form a seamless point of entry, improving visibility and reducing the opportunities for antisocial behaviour. New pathways were laid, leading visitors to such features as the Butterfly Walk, and seating was installed. The existing adventure playground was in poor condition; it was removed, creating sight lines across the park, and a new play area created, named after local park champion Anne Keane, using rubble from the former playground. An outdoor gym is also well used – indeed, the park has been transformed as a local amenity.

Dickens' Fields is also important in terms of nature conservation. Eleven bird species have been identified there, and it provides a vital stepping stone for birds moving across the borough's parks and open spaces.

Small in scale but significant for its impact on an area where open space is at a premium, the project was developed in consultation with local residents. A new play area and outdoor gym were part of a programme that included the closure of a road, new seating and reconfigured routes across the site.

SITE PLAN

Landscape

Sponsors

In addition to those listed on page 2, Merrell Publishers is grateful to the following sponsors:

MACCREANOR LAVINGTON

getliving

DELANCEY

BARRATT —LONDON—

Allies and Morrison

Also supported by:

GPE

dRMM

Index

Page numbers in *italic* refer to the illustrations.

18 Blackfriars Road 6, 9, *9*
53 and 55 Great Suffolk Street 69, 70–71, *70–71*
81–87 Weston Street 66, *66–7*
95 Peckham Road 10, 38, *38–9*
160 Tooley Street 84, *84–5*

A21 Architects 82, *82–3*
Aalto, Alvar 115
Ab Rogers Design 131
Abercrombie, Patrick 142
Adams, Maurice Bingham 130
Affinity Sutton Homes 10, 62
Alan Baxter Partnership 80
Albany Road 142
Albatross Way 100
Albion Street 40, 78
Albion Street Housing 10, 40–41, *40–41*
Allford Hall Monaghan Morris (AHMM) 10, 12, 50–53, *50–53*, 66, *66–7*, 84, *84–5*, 110, *110*, 134–5, 139
Allies and Morrison 9, 10, 64, 90, *90–91*, 94–5, *94–5*, 140–41, *140–41*
Alsop, Will 12, 13, 20, 24, 129
Alumno 26
AOC Architecture 10, 12, 86, 96, *96–7*, 117, *117*
Appleby Blue 37, 42, *42–3*
Arbor 90
Arcadis 80
Area 10 arts space 24
ARK All Saints Academy, Camberwell 12, 110, *110*
Art Nouveau 117
Arts and Crafts movement 72, 73
AustralianSuper 140
Aylesbury estate, Walworth 8, 10, 13, 34, 37, 76, 77, 133
Aylesbury Estate Block SO1, Walworth 46–8, *46–8*

Bakerloo line 94
Balfour Beatty 110
Bankside 6, 7, 8, 70
Bankside Hotel 58
Bankside Yards 9, 89, 90, *90–91*
Barratt London 100
Barry, Charles Jr 118
Battersea power station 32
BBC 34
Bell, Sir David 6
Bell Phillips 10, 30–31, *30–31*, 40–41, *40–41*, 133, 134, 136, *136–7*, 142–3, *142–3*
Bellenden Primary School 112, *112*
Bellenden Road 114
Berkeley Homes 144, 145
Bermondsey 8, 10, 11–12, 13, 20, 37, 42, 50, 109, 117
Bermondsey Conservation Area 44
Betjeman, Sir John 13–14, 80
Blackfriars 9
Blackfriars Bridge 58, 89, 90, 92
Blackfriars Circus 9, 89, 92, *92–3*
Blackfriars Road 58, 90, 92, 129
Blackfriars station 90
Blavatnik, Sir Leonard 32
Blavatnik Building, Tate Modern 14, 17, 32–3, *32–3*
Borough Market 15, 44
Brandon estate, Kennington 8
BREEAM ratings 127
Bridge Theatre 14–15, 144

British Land 10, 140
Broadgate 70
Brockham Street 146
Building Schools for the Future programme 11
The Buildings of England 8–9, 86, 96, 130
Burgess Park, Camberwell 113, 133, 142–3, 142–3
Burgess Park West, Camberwell 143
Burgess Sports 143

Camberwell 8, 12, 25, 133, 142
Camberwell College of Arts 109, 130–31, 130–31
Camberwell Green 13, 18
Camberwell Library 13, 18, 18–19
Camberwell New Road 110
Canada Dock 140, 141, 141
Canada Water 7, 8, 9–10, 13, 133, 140
Canada Water Jubilee line station 100, 140, 141
Canada Water Library 13, 20, 20–21, 40, 100
Canada Water Masterplan 140–41, 140–41
Canary Wharf 140
Castle Centre 22, 22–3
Castle Square 95
Chamberlin, Powell & Bon 11
Chapter London Bridge 14, 44, 44–5
Chapter Tower 9
Charcoalblue 26
Charing Cross Hospital 74
Cherry Garden School, Peckham 12, 114, 114
Cheung, Maria 60
China Wharf 20
Church of the English Martyrs 63
City Hall 7
City of London 6, 8
Clarence Centre for Enterprise and Innovation 13, 122–3, 122–3
Clarion Housing Group 10
Coffey Architects 10, 50–53, 50–53
Collado Collins 120–21, 120–21
Commission for Architecture and the Built Environment 104, 144
Cottrell & Vermeulen 112, 112
Creative Enterprise Zones 12, 25
Crouch End 24
The Cut 12, 13, 128
CZWG 13, 20, 20–21, 100

Davies, Dame Siobhan 28
Davey Street 113
Dawes Street 34
Deacon Street 136
Deal Porter Square 100
Delancey 94–5
Denmark Hill 82
Denmark Hill station 83
Dewar Street 112
Dickens' Fields 146, 146–7
Dock Shed 141
Donald Insall Associates 86
dRMM 10, 62, 136–8, 138
Duchess Walk 144
Duke of Clarence pub 123
Dulwich 8
Dulwich College Laboratory 118, 118–19
Dulwich Common 118
Duttson, Robin 60

Early Housing Sites (EHS) 10, 62
Eden Project, Cornwall 118
Eileen House 64
Elephant and Castle 8–9, 10, 12, 13, 22, 23, 28, 37, 60, 62, 64, 89, 134, 146
Elephant and Castle Opportunity Area 54, 86
Elephant and Castle Town Centre 94–5, 94–5
Elephant Park 7, 10, 86, 94, 133, 134–8, 134–9
Elephant Springs 7
Elliott Wood 78
Employment Academy 72, 72–3
English Heritage 58
Euston station 80
Eveline Lowe School, Bermondsey 116

Fabrix 70
Falmouth Road 146
Farmers Road 110
Feilden Clegg Bradley Studios 111, 111
Feix & Merlin 86–7, 86–7
Fetal Medicine Research Foundation 82
Fetal Medicine Research Institute 82, 82
Finnish Seamen's Church 40
Foster, Norman 6
Foster + Partners 8, 9, 9
The Founding 141
4Futures 115
Freshire Ltd 66

Gaunt Street 64
General Projects 27, 86, 87
Get Living 94
GLC Architects' Department 13
Globe Theatre 6, 15, 90
Goldsmiths, University of London 13, 26, 26
Gomm Road 30
Gough, Piers 20
Grand Press 141, 141
Grand Surrey Canal 143
Grange Road 50
Grant Associates 42, 136–7
Great Maze Pond 74
Great Portland Estates 84
Great Suffolk Street 70
Greater London Authority 8
Greater London Council (GLC) 11, 142
Greater London Plan (1944) 142
Greenland Dock 140
Greystar 44
Grimshaw 80–81, 80–81, 118, 118–19
Grove Lane 83
GTH Architects 128–9, 128–9
Guinness Partnership 63
Guy's and St Thomas' NHS Foundation Trust 74
Guy's Cancer Centre 74, 74–5

Haberdashers' Borough Academy 120–21, 120–21
Hadston Southwark Ltd 120
Hall, Edwin Thomas 72
Harold Moody Health Centre 76, 76–7
Harper Road 146
Harriet Hardy Extra Care 46, 46, 49, 49
Harris Birthright Centre 82
Havil Street 27, 72
Hawkins\Brown 12, 46, 70–71, 70–71, 114, 114, 140–41, 140–41
Hawkstone Road 111
Haworth Tompkins 14, 37, 63, 63
Heathrow airport 106
Herzog & de Meuron 14, 32–3, 32–3
Heygate estate 8, 10, 37, 62, 94, 133, 134–9
Heygate Street 139
Highshore School 110, 110
Hines and Lipton Rogers 6
Historic England 87, 104
Hitchmough, James 143
The Hithe 69, 78, 78–9
Holland Street 32, 56
Hopton's Almshouses 56
Howells 10, 100–2, 100–3
HTA Design 10, 34, 34–5, 46, 76
Hytner, Nicholas 14

Ian Ritchie Architects 144
I'Anson, Edward 54, 86
IF_DO 78, 78–9

Jarvis, Henry 86
Jestico + Whiles 13, 26, 26
John McAslan + Partners 13, 18, 18–19, 22, 22–3, 60
John Pardey Architects 11, 109, 116, 116
Joiner Street 91
Jonas, Dame Judith Mayhew 6
Jubilee Line Extension 13, 69

Keane, Anne 146
Kennington 8
King's College 44
King's College Hospital Campus 82, 82, 83
King's Reach Estates 98
King's Reach Tower 8
Kinnear Landscape Architects 30
KPF 8, 9, 15, 44, 44–5, 98, 98–9
Kubrick, Stanley 95
Kuropatwa Ltd 38, 92

LaLiT hotel 144
Lambeth 7
Lambeth Bridge 92
LDA Design 142–3, 142–3, 146, 146–7
Lendlease 10, 60, 134–9
Lewerentz, Sigurd 115
Liberty's 72
Lindenmayer, Aristid 118
Lipton, Sir Stuart 6
Loman Street 71
London Bridge 7, 106
London Bridge City 8
London Bridge House 104
London Bridge station 8, 13–14, 14, 44, 66, 68–9, 69, 80–81, 80–81, 84, 104, 106, 107
London Bridge Street 80, 104, 107
London College of Communication (LCC) 95, 95
London County Council (LCC) 11, 116, 142
London Overground 13, 140
London Plan (2021) 8, 9
London Road 13, 94, 124
London South Bank University (LSBU) 13, 64, 109, 122–3, 122–3, 124–7, 124–7
London Square 10, 37, 50–53, 50–53
London Theatre Company 14
London Underground 13, 91, 94, 95
London Wildlife Trust 141
Lowe, Eveline 116
Lower Marsh, Waterloo 78
LSBU Hub 13, 124–7, 124–7
Lyons Israel Ellis 11

Maccreanor Lavington 9, 92, 92–3, 138–9, 139
Mae 46–8
Maggie's Centre, Charing Cross Hospital 74
MAKE Architects 90, 90–91
Mandarin Oriental hotel 90
Manor Place 54
Manor Place Housing 54–5, 54–5
Maple Quays 100–2, 100–1
Marlborough Grove 116
Marson, Una 34
Maudsley Charity 83
Mayor of London 64

Index

Meanwhile Space 78
Medd, David and Mary 11, 116
Metropolitan Fire Brigade 120
Metropolitan Tabernacle 60, 61
Millennium Bridge 6, 7
Ministry of Sound 64
Monnow Road 117
More London 8, 15
Morgan Capital Partners 70
Morris + Company 76, 76–7, 83, 83
Mountford, E.W. 144
Mountview, Peckham 12, 17, 24–5, 24–5
Murray, Ward & Partners 130
Mylne, Robert 92

Nairn, Ian 8
National Heritage Lottery Fund 30
Native Land 56, 90
NCG Group 128
Neo Bankside 32, 56, 56–7
Network Rail 80
New Kent Road 94, 139
New York 6
Newington Butts 94
Newington Causeway 94
Newlands Academy, Peckham 12, 109, 115, 115
News Building 106, 106
News UK 106
NHS 76
Northern line 94
Notting Hill Genesis 54
Nunhead 8
Nunhead Green 10, 96, 96–7
Nunhead Green Community Centre 89
Nursery Row Park 63

Old Kent Road 8
Old Kent Road Opportunity Area 50
One Blackfriars 8, 37, 58, 58–9, 90
One the Elephant 9, 22, 60, 60–61
One Housing 96
One Tower Bridge 14, 144, 144–5
Ontario Point 100–2, 100–3
Ortus 83, 83
Otto Street 62

Palestra building 128
Panter Hudspith Architects 10, 11, 37, 62, 62

Paris 6
Park Central East, Elephant Park 139
Park Central West, Elephant Park 139
Peabody Trust 63
Peckham 8, 12, 17, 25, 109, 115, 131
Peckham Hill Street 24
Peckham Levels 12–13
Peckham Library 12, 13, 20, 24
Peckham Road 11, 13, 17, 38, 72, 130
Peckham Rye 112
Peter Barber Architects 10–11, 38, 38–9, 72, 72–3
Pevsner, Nikolaus 26, 96
Phoenix Primary School 11–12, 109, 116, 116
Piano, Renzo 104
Platform 5 Architects 128–9, 128–9
PLP Architecture 90, 90–91
Pollard Thomas Edwards 54–5, 54–5
Poor Law Guardians 72
Post-modernism 12, 96, 117
Potters Fields Park 144, 144–5
Printworks London 141, 141
PTAL 120–21, 120–21

Qatar 104
Queen Elizabeth Street 144

Randall-Page, Peter 118, 119
RIBA 10, 109, 111, 136
RIBA Stirling Prize 13, 20, 24
Rich industrial estate 50
Rivington Street Studio 13, 122
Rockingham estate 146
Rodney Road 63, 138
Rogers, Richard 56, 57
Rotherhithe 10, 40, 69, 78, 140
Rotherhithe Primary School 7, 109, 111, 111
Rotherhithe Tunnel 40
Royal Road 10, 11, 37, 62
Royal Road Housing 62, 62
RPBW Architects 8, 69, 104–7, 104–7, 106
RSHP 32, 56, 56–7, 74, 74–5
Rye Lane 12–13

St Gabriel Walk 22, 60
St George (developer) 58
St George's Circus 9, 13, 92, 93, 122, 123
St George's Circus Conservation Area 92, 122
St George's Road 28, 94
St George's Way 142
St Mary's church, Elephant and Castle 22
St Michael and All Angels Academy 110
St Michael's church 110, 110
St Olave's church 40
St Paul's Cathedral 6, 32
St Peter's church 48
St Thomas Street 91
Sarah Wigglesworth Architects 28, 28–9
Sayer Street 136
Schwartz, Martha 60
Scott, Giles Gilbert 32, 33
Second World War 8, 94, 109, 142, 144, 146
Seifert, Richard 8, 98, 99, 104
Sellar, Irvine 104
Sellar Property Group 104, 106, 107
SEND (Special Educational Needs or Disabilities) programme 12, 109, 114, 115
Shackleton, Ernest 118
Shakespeare's Globe Theatre 6, 15, 90
Shangri-La hotel 104–6
The Shard 8, 9, 15, 44, 69, 89, 91, 104–7, 104–5
Shard Place 107, 107
The Shard Quarter 104–7, 104–7
Shawcross, Conrad 118
SILS3 Pupil Referral Unit 7, 113, 113
SimpsonHaugh 8, 58, 58–9
Siobhan Davies Dance Studios 17, 28, 28–9
Sivetidis, Dr Savas 6
Soane, John 48
Solidspace 66
South Gardens, Elephant Park 138–9, 139
South London College 144
South London Gallery 130
Southbank 56
Southbank Centre 90

Southbank Tower 8, 98, 98–9
Southwark Bridge 92
Southwark Bridge Road 64, 120
Southwark Cathedral 15, 44
Southwark College 12, 13, 128–9, 128–9
Southwark Council 9–10, 12, 13, 18, 24, 34, 50, 54, 58, 63, 64, 69, 72, 78, 84, 86, 96, 109, 128, 144, 146
Southwark Park 111
Southwark Park Pavilion 30–31, 30–31
Southwark Park Road 42
Southwark Street 56, 90
Southwark Studios 50
Southwark Towers 104
Southwark Town Hall 26, 26–7
Spa School, Bermondsey 12, 117, 117
Squire & Partners 9, 60, 60–61, 144, 144–5
Stamford Street 98
Stansfield Smith, Sir Colin 116
Starr, Nick 14
Stead Street 63
Stead Street Housing 37, 63, 63
Stephen Marshall Architects 130–31, 130–31
Stiff + Trevillion 90, 90–91
Stirling and Gowan 11
Stuart Road 115
Sumner Street 32
Surrey Docks 69, 100, 140
Surrey Quays Road 20, 100
Surrey Quays station 140

Tannery Arts 50, 52
Tate Modern 6, 7, 14, 15, 17, 32–3, 32–3, 56, 90
Thames, River 32, 90, 106
Thames Reach 11, 72
Thameslink 80
Theatre Peckham 13, 26, 26–7
Thurlow Street 34, 35, 76
Tim Ronalds Architects 113, 113
Tooley Street 80, 84, 91, 144, 145
Tower Bridge 144

Tower Bridge Road 144, 145
Townshend Landscape Architects 140–41, 140–41
TP Bennett 80, 104
Trafalgar Place, Elephant Park 10, 136–8, 138
The Tree House, Elephant Park 7, 133, 134, 136, 136–7
Trinity Church Square 146
Trollope, Anthony 42
Turner Works 12–13, 24–5, 24–5
Two Fifty One 9, 37, 64, 64–5

Una Marson Library 13, 20, 34, 34–5
United St Saviour's Charity 42
University of the Arts London (UAL) 95, 130, 131
Upper Ground 98
Urban Strategies Inc. 100

Vauxhall Pleasure Gardens 31

Walworth 10, 13, 34, 46–9, 69
Walworth estate 63
Walworth Road 86, 87, 94, 139
Walworth Town Hall and Central Library 69, 86–7, 86–7
Waterloo Bridge 92
Weber Industries 78
West End 140
West Grove 139
Westminster Bridge 92
Westmoreland Road 47
Weston Street 44, 66
WilkinsonEyre 13, 124–7, 124–7
Winchester House 120–21, 121
Windsor Walk 82
Witherford Watson Mann Architects 42, 42–3
Wright & Wright 109, 115, 115
WSP 80
Wyndham Road 110

Young Vic 128
YRM 40

Zogolovitch, Roger 66

Acknowledgements

I am grateful to Hugh Merrell, for commissioning this book; to my editor, Rosanna Fairhead, a constant source of help and support; to Nicola Bailey, for the design of the book; and to Nick Wheldon for assembling the many photographs and drawings. Richard Wells was the ever-helpful coordinator at Southwark Council, where Michael Tsoukaris, Catherine Brownell, John Ryan and Colin Wilson also provided invaluable advice. Finally, thanks are due to the many architectural practices who tirelessly answered queries and provided me with information on their projects.

Publisher's Acknowledgements

Merrell Publishers is grateful to Lord Foster, Kieron Williams, Richard Wells, Michael Tsoukaris, Steve Platts, Kate van Rijswijk, Sarah Christophers, Herbie Christophers and Galiema Amien-Cloete for their help in the making of this book.

Picture Credits

l = left, r = right, t = top, c = centre, b = bottom

© Alan Williams Photography: 128r, 129tl, tr, b; © Alan Williams Photography/GTH Architects: 12; © Allford Hall Monaghan Morris: 66t, b, 84t, tc, bc, 110b; © Allies and Morrison: 64t, b, 65tl, 94t, b, 95t, bl, br; © AOC Architecture: 96t, b, 117tr; © APS (UK)/Alamy Stock Photo: 124t; © Argus/Alamy Stock Photo: 15; © James Balston: 145tl; © Bell Phillips Architects: 30br, 40t, bl, br, 136t, 143cr; © Alex Bland/Arcaid Images: 33tl, r, bl; Courtesy British Land: 141tl, r, cl, bl; © James Brittain: 115tr, cl, bl, br; © Richard Bryant/Arcaid Images: 28t, 29tl, tr, bl, br; © Matt Clayton: 35t, b; © Phil Coffey/Coffey Architects: 52b, 53l, r; © Coffey Architects: 52t; © Anthony Coleman: 108–9, 112tr, cr, br; © Cottrell & Vermeulen: 112l; © Tim Crocker: 20b, 21tl, tr, cl, cr, bl, 24tl, tr, 25tr, b, 47tl, r, bl, 48b, 49t, b, 93tl, tr, bl, 139l, r; © CZWG architects: 20t, c; © Michel Denancé: 105, 106tl; © dRMM: 138bl, br; © Philip Durrant: 57br; © Philipp Ebeling: 36–7, 43bl, br; © Eleventh Hour Photography/Alamy Stock Photo: 65bl; © Greg Balfour Evans/Alamy Stock Photo: 31b; © Robert Evans/Alamy Stock Photo: 65r; © Liz Eve/fotohaus: 130b, 131t, bl, br; © Feilden Clegg Bradley Studios: 111t; © Feix & Merlin Architects: 86t, b, 87tr, br; © Foster + Partners: 9; © Grain London: 91cr, b; © David Grandorge: 117l, cr, br; © Grimshaw: 80tl, 81t, 118b, 119bl; Courtesy Grimshaw/Network Rail: 80b; © GTH Architects: 128bl; © GTH Architects/Platform 5 Architects: 128tl; © Hawkins\Brown: 70tl, 114tr, br; © Hawkins\Brown/Darcstudio: 71t, b; © Haworth Tompkins: 63t; © Herzog & de Meuron: 32t, b; © Jack Hobhouse: 83t, c, br, 114l, tcr, bcr; © Andrew Holt: 7; © Fred Howarth: 63c, bl, br; © Howells: 101tl, 102tr, br; © HTA Design: 24t, b; © Hufton + Crow: 59t, bl, cr, 107tl, 111ct, cb, bl, br; © IF_DO: 78t, c, b; © Cannon Ivers/LDA Design: 142t, b, 143tl, tr; © Jason Hawkes Photography: cover; © Jestico + Whiles/Matt Clayton: 26t, 27t, bl, br; © Jestico + Whiles: 26b; © John McAslan and Partners: 18t, 22t, c, b, 23b; © John Pardey Architects: 116t; © James Jones: 60b, 61tl, tr, bl, br, 144c, b, 145tr, b; © Simon Kennedy: 122t, 123t, bl, br; © Kohn Pedersen Fox: 45tl, bl, 99bl; © Natalie Lawrence/Lendlease: 138tr; © LDA Design: 146; © Benedict Luxmore: 100, 101tr, bl, br, 102l, 103; © Maccreanor Lavington: 92t, b, 93br, 134t; Mae: 46t, b, 48t; © Mike Massaro, courtesy IF_DO: 79tl, tr, bl, br; © Morris+Company: 76t, c, 83bl;

© James Morris: 116l, r, b; © Mozses: 44t, b, 45r; © Luke O'Donovan: 54tr, 55t, b; © Kilian O'Sullivan: 16–17, 136b, 137tl, tr, b, 132–3, 143br; © Kilian O'Sullivan/Bell Phillips Architects: 30t, bl, 31t; © Panter Hudspith Architects: 62t; © Pennie Withers Photography: 120, 121l, r; © Peter Barber Architects: 38t, b, 39bl, 72t, c; © PLP Architecture: 88–9, 90, 91tr; © Pollard Thomas Edwards: 54tl, b; © Paul Raftery: 14, 68–9, 81cl, cr; © RPBW – Renzo Piano Building Workshop Architects: 104l, r, 106tr, b, 107r, bl; © Alex de Rijke/dRMM: 138tl; © Rivington Street Studio: 122c, b; © RSHP: 56b, 74t, b; © James Santer, courtesy of AHMM: 50b, 51tl, tr, bl, br; © Agnese Sanvito: 80tr, 81b; © Sarah Wigglesworth Architects: 28c, b; © Adam Scott: 82t, bl, br; © Daniel Shearing: 118t, 119t, cl, br; © SimpsonHaugh: 58t, b; Photography: Tian Khee Siong: 87tl, bl; © Secchi Smith: 41t, b; © Tim Soar: 67l, tr, cr, br, 84b, 85tl, tr, bl, br, 97tl, bl, br, 98, 99tl, tr, br, 110t, tcl, bcl, br, 134b, 135tl, tr, bl, br; © Neil Speakman for LDA Design: 147tl, tr, b; © Michael Squire/Squire & Partners: 144t; © Squire & Partners: 60t; © Andy Stagg: 77t, cl, cr; © Stephen Marshall Architects: 130tl, tr; © Jim Stephenson: 70tr, bl, br, 113tr, br; © Graham Stirk/RSHP: 56t; © Edmund Sumner: 57t, bl, 76b; © Edmund Sumner/VIEW: 124b, 125tr, br, 126–7; © Edmund Sumner – View/Alamy Stock Photo: 19tl, tr, bl, cr, br; © THP Photo Imaging: 59br; © Tim Ronalds Architects: 113l; © Townshend Landscape Architects: 140; © Simon Turner/Alamy Stock Photo: 18b, 23t; © Turner Works: 24b; © Uniform Communications Limited/Allford Hall Monaghan Morris: 50t; © Enrique Verdugo: 11; © Philip Vile: 43tl, tr, cl, cr; © Philip Vile/Haworth Tompkins: 2; © Morley von Sternberg: 39t, br, 62c, b, 72b, 73tl, tr, b, 75tl, tr, bl, br; © Wilkinson Eyre: 125tl, bl; © Wire Collective: 91tl; © Witherford Watson Mann Architects: 42t, bl, br; © Wright & Wright Architects: 115tl; © Simon Yeung: 25tl

The publisher has made every effort to trace and contact the copyright holders of the images reproduced in this book. It will be happy to correct in subsequent editions any errors or omissions that are brought to its attention.

First published 2025 by
Merrell Publishers Limited,
London and New York

Merrell Publishers Limited
70 Cowcross Street
London EC1M 6EJ

merrellpublishers.com

Text copyright © 2025 Kenneth Powell,
except page 6: © 2025 Lord Foster; and page 7:
© 2025 Kieron Williams
Design and layout copyright © 2025 Merrell
Publishers Limited
Illustrations copyright © the copyright holders;
see page 151

All rights reserved. No part of this publication
may be reproduced, stored in a retrieval
system or transmitted, in any form or by any
means, electronic, mechanical, photocopying,
recording or otherwise, without the prior written
permission of the publisher.

British Library Cataloguing-in-Publication data:
A catalogue record for this book is available from
the British Library.

ISBN 978-1-8589-4717-4

Produced by Merrell Publishers Limited
Designer: Nicola Bailey
Project editor: Rosanna Fairhead
Picture researcher: Nick Wheldon
Proofreader: Barbara Roby
Indexer: Hilary Bird

Printed and bound in China

Page 2: Bridge Theatre (see pages 14–15)
Pages 16–17: Southwark Park Pavilion (page 30)
Pages 36–7: Appleby Blue (page 42)
Pages 68–9: London Bridge Station (page 80)
Pages 108–9: Bellenden School (page 112)
Pages 132–33: Elephant Park (page 134)

Kenneth Powell is an architecture critic, journalist and writer. He has published widely, including books on Norman Foster, Richard Rogers and John McAslan, as well as *New Architecture in Britain* (2003), *City Reborn* (2004), *New London Architecture* (2005) and *New London Architecture 2* (2007; with Cathy Strongman), all by Merrell. He was elected Honorary Fellow of the RIBA in 2000.